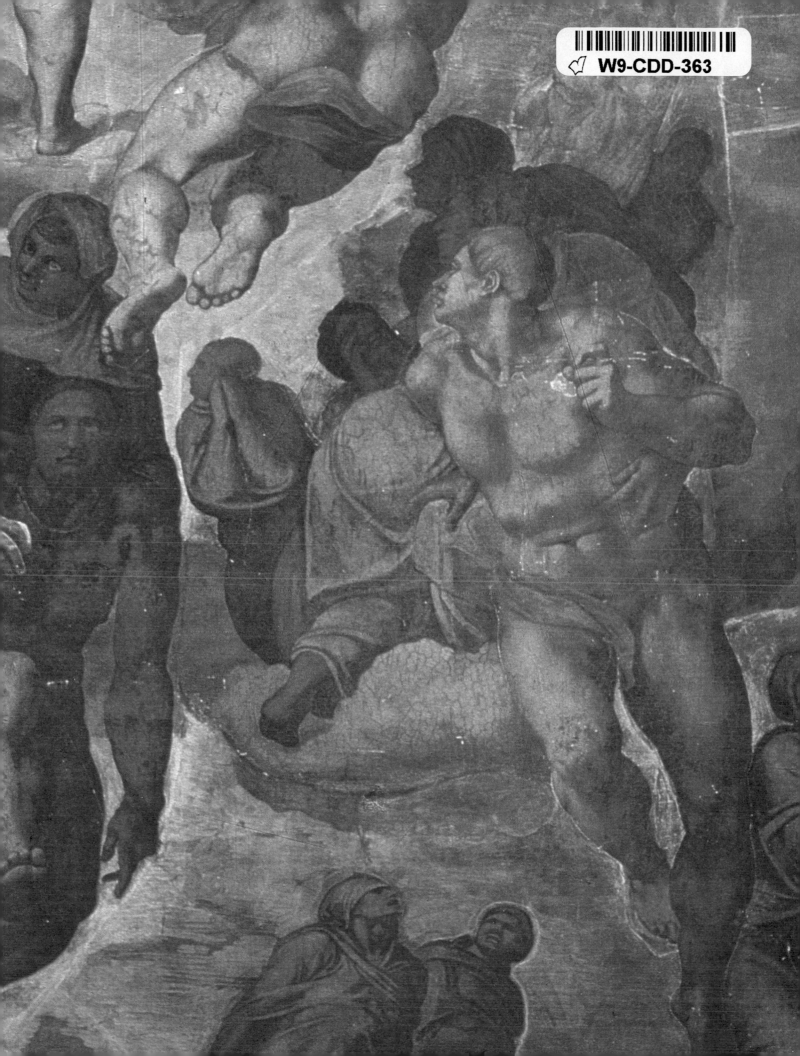

Michelangelo

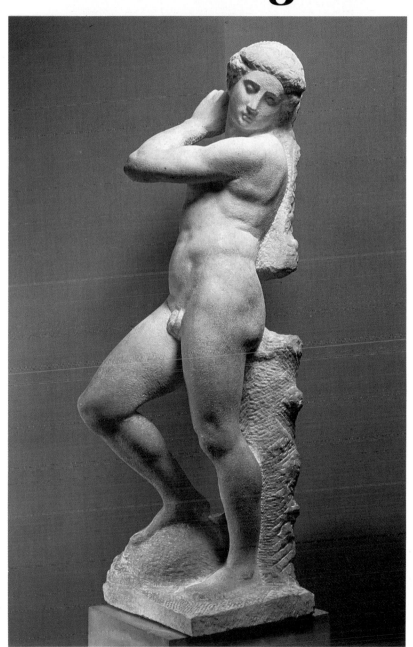

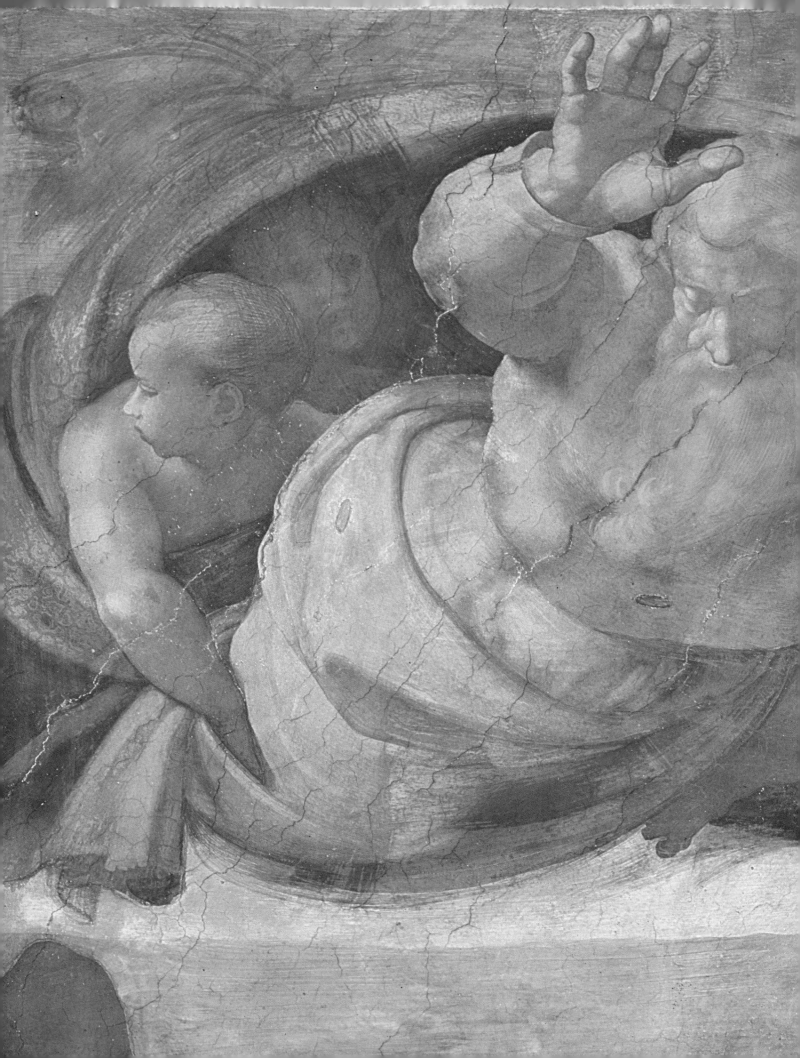

Michelangelo

Jeffery Daniels

CHARTWELL
BOOKS, INC.

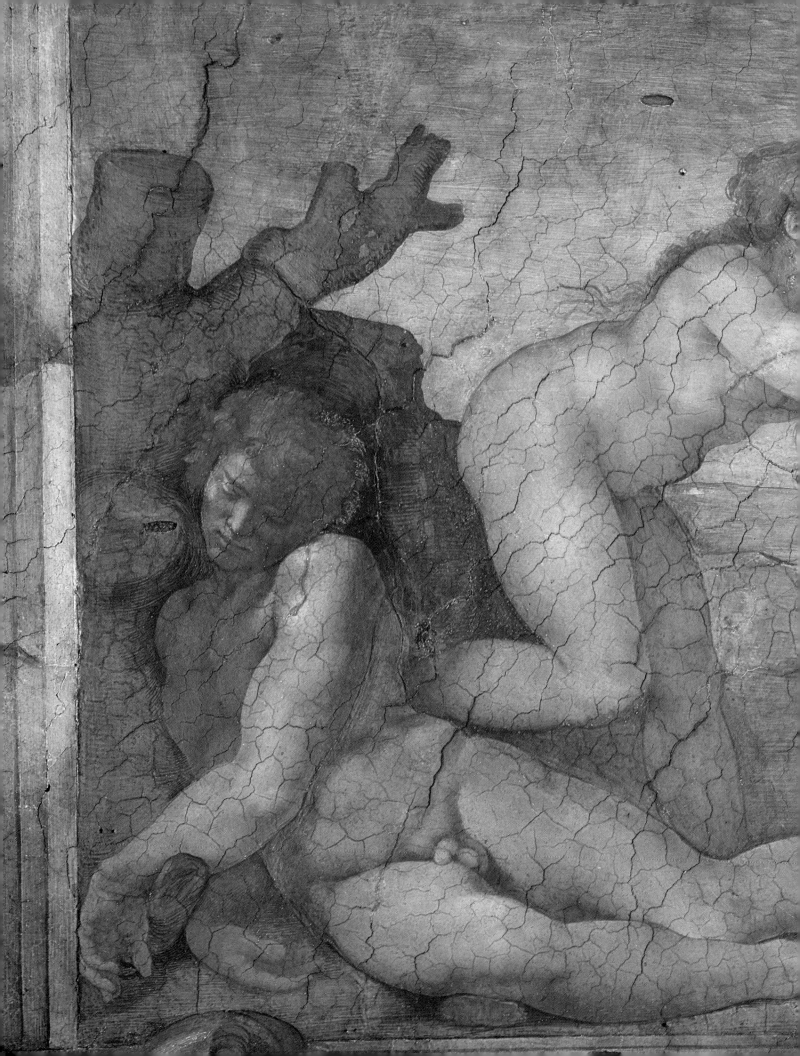

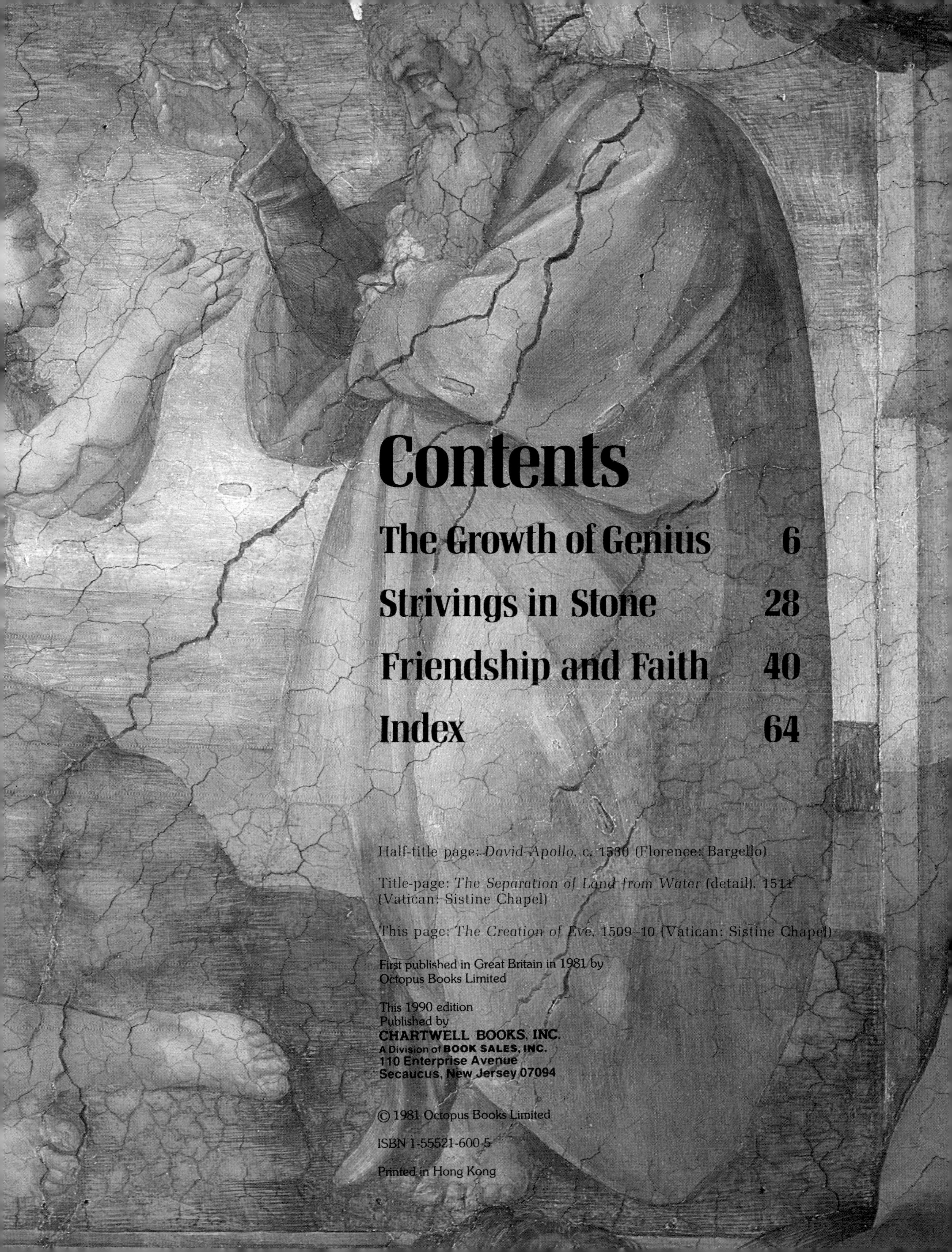

Contents

Half-title page: *David Apollo*, c. 1530 (Florence: Bargello)

Title-page: *The Separation of Land from Water (detail)*, 1511 (Vatican: Sistine Chapel)

This page: *The Creation of Eve*, 1509–10 (Vatican: Sistine Chapel)

First published in Great Britain in 1981 by
Octopus Books Limited

This 1990 edition
Published by
CHARTWELL BOOKS, INC.
A Division of BOOK SALES, INC.
110 Enterprise Avenue
Secaucus, New Jersey 07094

© 1981 Octopus Books Limited

ISBN 1-55521-600-5

Printed in Hong Kong

The Growth of Genius

'Truly his coming was to the world . . . an exemplar sent by God to the men of our arts, to the end that they might learn from his life the nature of noble character, and from his works what true and excellent craftsmen ought to be.'

This quotation comes from the *Life* of Michelangelo written by his friend and fellow artist Giorgio Vasari. Although the book was published more than four hundred years ago the fundamental point is still true today: that Michelangelo possessed, to a degree rarely equalled and certainly never surpassed, creative ability so outstanding and wide ranging as to command universal admiration, both during his own lifetime and ever since.

Michelangelo di Lodovico Buonarroti Simoni was born in 1475 at Caprese, not far from Arezzo, but shortly afterwards the family moved closer to Florence, to a farm at Settignano, a village famous for its quarries of that warm brownish grey stone known as *pietra serena*. The infant's wet nurse was the wife of a stone cutter, with whose milk, Michelangelo told Vasari, he 'sucked in . . . the chisels and hammer with which I make my figures'. Italy in the late 15th century was not a unified country but a collection of separate city states, each ruled by a powerful family. Florence was no exception, being dominated by the Medici, who were at first careful to respect the republican constitution of the city but soon revealed their dynastic ambitions, eventually becoming dukes in 1537 and finally grand dukes in 1569. It was Lorenzo de' Medici, known as 'the magnificent', who became Michelangelo's first patron, but before that he had spent a short period in the Florentine workshop of Domenico Ghirlandaio (1449–94), from whom he learnt the difficult technique of painting in fresco on wet plaster. This was to prove invaluable later on in his career, although he tried to conceal the fact of this apprenticeship, because he felt that it detracted from his image as a self-taught genius.

In fact he seems to have spent less than a year in Ghirlandaio's workshop before being transferred to a school set up in the Medici gardens by Lorenzo himself, who appointed the aged but distinguished sculptor Bertoldo di Giovanni as its keeper and teacher. Michelangelo was one of his most diligent pupils, studying the examples of ancient sculpture with such careful attention that he was able to produce what passed for genuine antiquities. His obvious ability attracted the particular notice of Lorenzo, who took the young sculptor into his own household, where he was treated as a member of the family. However, such favour inevitably aroused the envy of fellow students, one of whom, Pietro Torrigiano, earned himself perpetual infamy in Florence by striking Michelangelo on the face and breaking his nose, a disfigurement from which he suffered much mental anguish. Torrigiano was banished and Michelangelo pursued his studies both in the garden and outside, spending many months copying Masaccio's frescoes in the church of the Carmine and creating his first original works in marble, of which two survive, the *Madonna of the Stairs* and the *Battle of the Centaurs*, eloquent testimony to the genius of the young prodigy. Lorenzo, who epitomizes the spirit of the Renaissance, that rebirth of civilization inspired by the achievements of the ancient Greeks and Romans, which began in Florence, died in 1492, to be succeeded by his son Piero. He proved himself totally inadequate to cope with the responsibility of office and was driven out by the people, infuriated by his cowardly submission to the French, who in 1494 had invaded Italy. During Piero's brief period of power, Michelangelo studied anatomy by dissecting corpses in the

The Madonna of the Stairs
*c.*1491
Marble
55.5 × 40 cm (21¾ × 15¾ in)
Florence: Casa Buonarroti

This delicate small-scale relief is Michelangelo's earliest surviving work, executed while he was studying in Lorenzo de' Medici's sculpture garden under the general guidance of Bertoldo, who had been a pupil of the famous sculptor Donatello (*c.*1386–1466). Describing it, Vasari states categorically that Michelangelo, 'wishing to counterfeit the manner of Donatello, he acquitted himself so well that it seems as if by Donatello's hand, save that there may be seen in it more grace and more design'. It should be regarded as a personal statement by the young artist since it was not the outcome of any commission.

The subject is superficially straightforward: the Virgin cradles the sleeping Christ child against her breast, from which He has drawn sustenance, while in the background four children play with a piece of cloth. It is heavy with symbolic meaning, however, as the cloth may have been intended to represent the shroud in which the dead Christ's body was wrapped, and the five steps on the left have been interpreted as either the mysteries of the rosary or the five letters of Mary's name in Latin (Maria).

Michelangelo's interest in ancient sculpture finds expression here both in the Virgin's classically Greek profile and the powerful back of the Christ child who could almost be an infant Hercules.

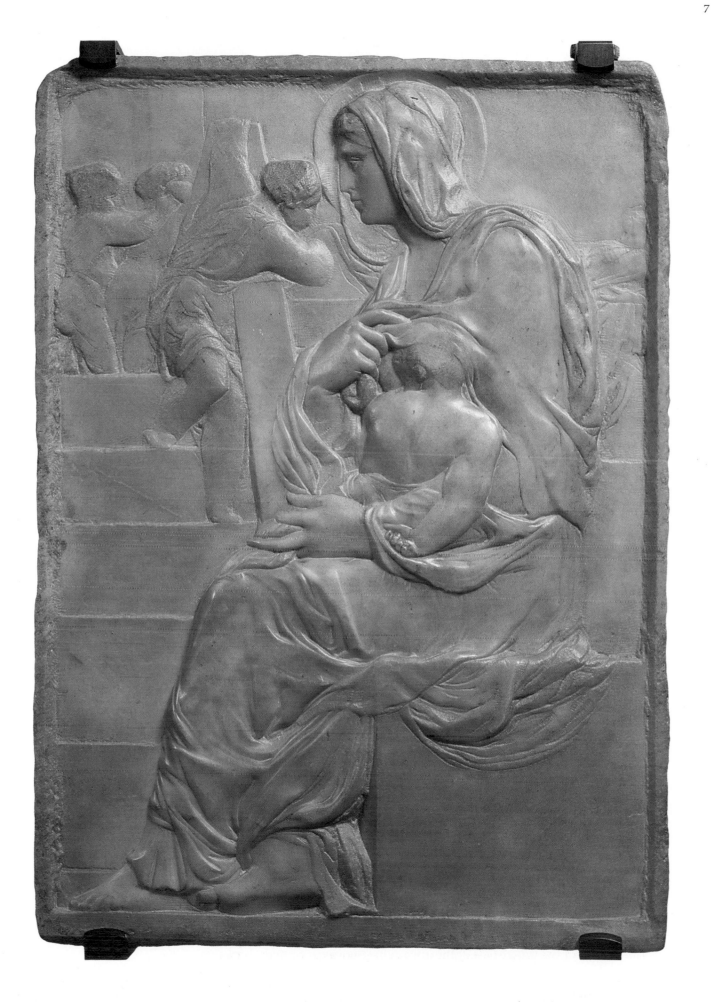

monastery of S. Spirito, for whose prior he carved, as a token of gratitude for the facility, a wooden *Crucifix*, which may well be the one rediscovered there in 1963.

Foreseeing the downfall of Piero, Michelangelo made his way to Bologna and then to Venice, returning once more to Bologna, where he found a protector and patron in the person of Giovanni Francesco Aldrovandi. Aldrovandi commissioned him to carve three small figures for the tomb of St Dominic in the church of S. Domenico, of which by far the most important is the beautiful *Angel with a Candlestick*. Returning to Florence, which was now wholly under the influence of the fanatical monk, Girolamo Savonarola, in whose puritanical eyes the arts were mere 'vanity', Michelangelo re-established contact with a younger branch of the Medici family in the persons of Lorenzo di Pierfrancesco and his brother Giovanni, in whose house he seems to have lived. There he carved a *Young St John the Baptist* which has been identified as the figure in the Bargello in Florence (as by Donatello), although there is no general agreement. The somewhat tormented quality of the work in question is utterly different from the calm assurance of the *Angel* in Bologna or the aggressive sensuality of the *Bacchus*, his first undoubted masterpiece, produced soon after his arrival in Rome. Vasari relates how Michelangelo, while still in Florence, had produced a *Sleeping Cupid* which was sold, as a genuine antiquity, through a dealer to Cardinal Riario di San Giorgio in Rome (a nephew of Pope Sixtus IV). Although the Cardinal refused to keep the figure and insisted on having his money returned when the deception was revealed, he was so curious to meet its creator that he summoned Michelangelo to Rome. Whether these were the precise circumstances of his departure from Florence is less relevant than the undeniable fact that Savonarola's 'gloomy theocracy' can have provided little scope for an aspiring young artist. Therefore, it must have been with a mixture of relief and excitement that Michelangelo set off in June 1496 for Rome, armed with a letter of introduction to Cardinal Riario from Lorenzo di Pierfrancesco.

The contrast between Florence under Savonarola and Rome under the Borgia Pope, Alexander VI, could hardly have been more pointed: Pintoricchio had recently completed his cycle of frescoes in the Borgia Apartments in the Vatican and his new patron, Cardinal Riario, was having an enormous palace built out of his winnings from a night's gambling with another papal nephew. It was Riario who seems to have commissioned the *Bacchus*, although Vasari categorically states that 'he did not commission Michelangelo to do anything' and attributes it to the man who certainly acquired it, the wealthy banker Jacopo Galli, in whose garden it was installed, among the pieces of antique sculpture of which he had an important collection. The young Michelangelo took every opportunity to study the principal collections of such works in Rome, with the result that his own technique benefited greatly. Although the *Bacchus* perfectly demonstrates this, it is nevertheless disconcertingly 'modern' in its unashamed sensuality. The rounded form of the figure conveys not only the effects of self indulgence in bodily pleasures, but also the effeminacy which is traditionally associated with his appearance. It is also worth noting that the figure is meant to be seen from all angles, so that the fine muscular back is as highly finished as the front.

Galli was the intermediary between Michelangelo and the French Cardinal Jean Bilhères de Lagraulas for the *Pietà*, which he intended to adorn his tomb in St Peter's, and for which Michelangelo was choosing marble in Carrara in the spring of 1498. It was probably finished at the very beginning of the new century, by which time the patron was already dead, and the sculptor was preparing to return to Florence where Savonarola had been ousted and executed and Michelangelo's enthusiastic supporter Piero Soderini now wielded power.

The bait which tempted him was the likelihood of being given the gigantic damaged block of marble which belonged to the Board of Works of Florence Cathedral and out of which it had originally been intended to carve a statue for one of the buttresses of the apse. Now Soderini wanted

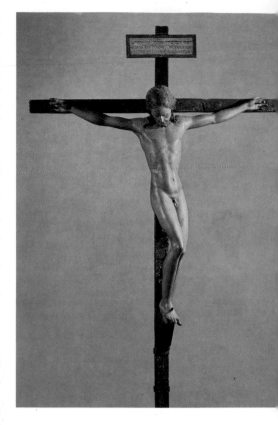

Above
Crucifix
1492–3
Wood, painted
134.6 cm (53 in) high
Florence: Casa Buonarroti

Whether this is in fact the crucifix that Michelangelo carved for the high altar of the Hospital of Santo Spirito is a matter for speculation. It remained there until 1600, when the altar was redesigned by Giovanni Caccini, for the Michelozzi family, when it was removed.

The identification of the crucifix illustrated as the missing Michelangelo has been accepted by many scholars, including Frederick Hartt who sees the 'slender proportions of the relatively soft and almost feminine figure' as characteristic of the 'lyrical, dreamy side of Michelangelo's nature'. Alessandro Parronchi, however, maintains that not only is it wrong stylistically, but that its dimensions are too small to accord with Condivi's statement (1553) that it was 'rather less than life size'.

One of the stronger arguments in favour of the Santo Spirito version is that it has always been in the building. Another is that, working in an uncharacteristic material, it is not entirely surprising that Michelangelo should work in an uncharacteristic style.

Right
The Battle of the Centaurs
1491–2
Marble
84.5 × 90.5 cm (33¼ × 35⅝ in)
Florence: Casa Buonarroti

This unfinished carving, in very high
relief, may have been begun for
Lorenzo the Magnificent, whose
death (in April 1492) could be the
reason for its incomplete state.
Michelangelo never parted with it
and it remained in the possession of
the Buonarroti family.

The subject is taken from a story
by the Roman poet Ovid, who
relates how, at the wedding feast of
Pirithous, King of the Lapiths and
Hippodamia, the centaurs (creatures
half man and half horse), inflamed
by wine, threw themselves upon the
female guests. This precipitated a
bloody battle in which the hero
Theseus played a part. Michelangelo
has used this dramatic episode as a
pretext for portraying the male nude
in violent action, thus indicating at
an early age the subject that was to
occupy him for much of his life and
dominate European painting for a
century.

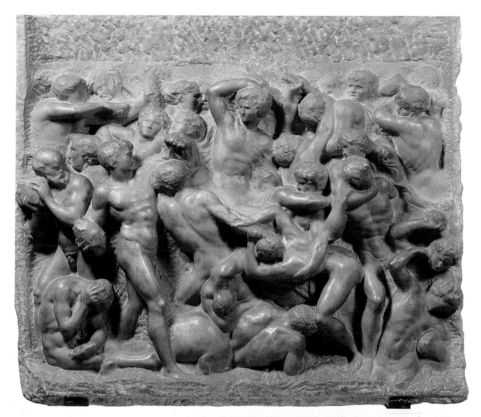

Right
An Angel with a Candlestick
1494–5
Marble
56.5 cm (22¼ in) high
Bologna: San Domenico

During his exile in Bologna in
1494–5, Michelangelo carved three
small figures for the shrine of St
Dominic, in the church of that name:
they are two saints, Petronius and
Proculus, and this angel, which
balances one by Niccolo dell' Arca
who had died earlier in the year.
The contrast between the sturdy yet
graceful figure by Michelangelo and
the conventional cuteness of
Niccolo's demonstrates perfectly the
difference between the early phase
of the Renaissance and the brief but
dazzling period which followed and
is known as the High Renaissance.
Even on such a small scale
Michelangelo could endow his angel
with monumentality and an
extraordinary sense of authority.
The soft, almost wax-like surface
seems, perhaps paradoxically, to
suggest the blurring effect of
movement, as if this divine
messenger had just landed.

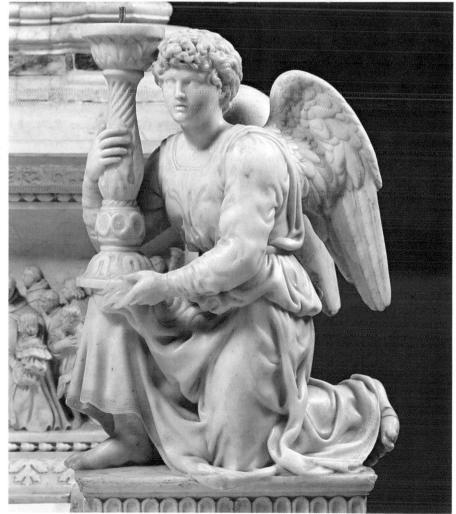

a figure that would somehow symbolize the restored republic and, after examining the marble, Michelangelo produced some small wax models of a *David* which he claimed that he could carve from it, without needing to add anything. Just as the *Pietà* made his reputation in Rome, so the great *David* established him as without rival in his native Florence.

During the four years that he spent in Florence Michelangelo also carved the *Bruges Madonna*, two *tondi* (circular compositions) for the Pitti and Taddei families and another, which was painted not carved, for the wedding of Agnolo Doni and Maddalena Strozzi. Just before signing the contract for the *David* he had committed himself to producing 15 small statues for the Piccolomini altar in Siena cathedral, but only four were finished, with the help of assistants. Having clearly lost interest in the project, he abandoned it in 1504. A joint commission from the Board of Works of Florence Cathedral, together with the Wool Guild, for 12 Apostles for the cathedral produced only the unfinished *St Matthew*, since it was interrupted by another commission, once again from Soderini, which, although abortive, proved to be much more significant. This was for a huge fresco to decorate one wall of the Great Council Hall of the Palazzo della Signoria, the offices of the city's governing body, where Leonardo da Vinci was already at work on a similar project.

He and Michelangelo disliked each other heartily but there is no reason to suppose that they met on site, since Michelangelo worked on the full-size preparatory drawing (called a 'cartoon') in a room which he was allocated at the Dyers' Hospital. The subject was the *Battle of Cascina* and, although the original cartoon was dismembered later in the century by the artists who were permitted to study it, a copy of the central section was made by Aristotile da Sangallo, and is preserved in Viscount Coke's collection at Holkham Hall, Norfolk. In spite of its short life, the *Cartoon of Pisa*, as it is often called, was enormously influential and figures from it can be spotted in many of the works by other painters.

That the cartoon was never translated into paint was due to the exercise of pressure by the new Pope, Julius II della Rovere, who summoned Michelangelo ('with much graciousness' according to Vasari) to Rome to begin work on the undertaking that was to cause him nearly 40 years of worry and strain, the Pope's own tomb, which he envisaged as one of the focal points of a new St Peter's. Michelangelo returned to Rome in March 1505, moving back to Carrara for most of the rest of the year to select marble for the Tomb, which he arranged to have transported by sea to Rome, where he himself took up residence in January 1506.

Having spent his own money in paying for the marble, Michelangelo called upon the Pope to obtain reimbursement, instead of which, as he complains in a letter dated 2 May 1506, he 'was turned out of doors, that is chased away', whereupon he immediately left Rome and returned to Florence. Eventually the two proud, obstinate men were reconciled at Bologna, to which the Pope had travelled at the head of his army, with the aim of re-establishing papal authority, weakened under Alexander VI. There he pardoned Michelangelo and commissioned from him a colossal bronze statue 'in the likeness of Pope Julius', which was eventually set up on the façade of the church of S. Petronio as a warning to the restive Bolognese, who destroyed it as soon as they dared, only a few years later.

Summoned once more to Rome by the Pope, Michelangelo was astonished and dismayed to be required not to continue with his work on the tomb, but to paint the ceiling of the Sistine Chapel. This was largely, according to Vasari, as a result of a plot hatched between Bramante, the Pope's architect, and Raphael, both of whom were envious of his matchless ability as a sculptor and hoped that he would disgrace himself when compelled to turn his hand to painting. They were certainly proved wrong when the scaffolding was finally removed in 1512, and the ceiling is almost certainly Michelangelo's greatest achievement, representing as it does that moment of perfect balance between the teachings of the Christian Church and the message conveyed by the tangible evidence of the ancient world: the beauty of the human body is accepted as the mirror of the soul, and not as its antithesis.

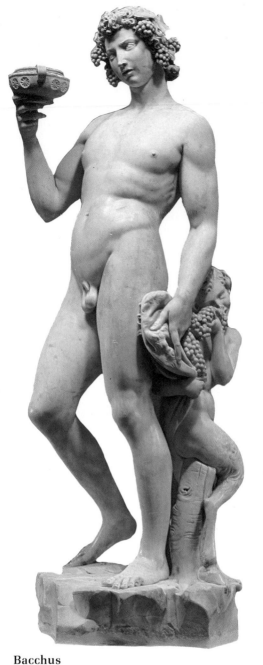

Bacchus
c. 1496–8
Marble
202.5 cm (79$\frac{5}{8}$ in) high
Florence: Museo Nazionale (Bargello)

Executed in Rome, where it was displayed in the gardens of Jacopo Galli, it was acquired in 1571–2 by Francesco de' Medici, second Grand Duke of Tuscany. He had it sent to Florence, where it has remained ever since, apart from a brief exile in Germany during World War 2.

It depicts the young god of wine, Bacchus, who has clearly already drunk deeply, accompanied by a young faun (half human, half goat) who laughingly nibbles at a large bunch of grapes. Bacchus gazes somewhat blearily at the wine cup in his right hand, and his parted lips suggest that he is about to take another draught.

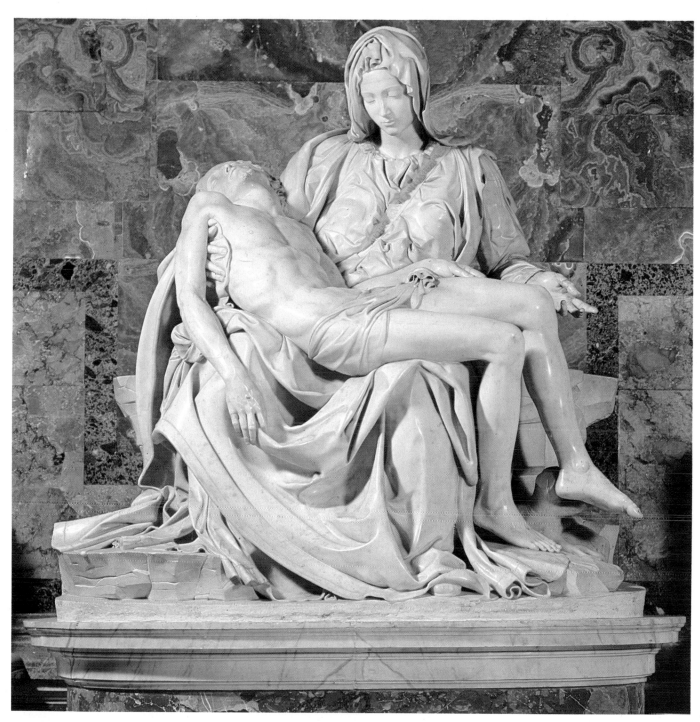

The Rome Pietà
1498–1500
Marble
174 × 195 cm (68½ × 76¾ in)
Rome: St Peter's

When Jacopo Galli, who owned the
Bacchus, drew up the contract for
this *Pietà* with the elderly French
cardinal who was commissioning it,
he promised that it would be 'the
most beautiful work in marble that
exists today in Rome'. Most people
would agree that this promise was
amply fulfilled. The group has
occupied several sites in St Peter's,

but since 1749 it has been in the
first chapel on the right of the nave.
    The Italian word 'pietà' means
'pity' and 'piety' at the same time,
but in religious art it has been given
a very precise meaning, as a
representation of the Virgin grieving
over the dead Christ. Although the
word is Italian, the origin of the
subject is northern European, so
that it is probable that the patron
chose it, rather than Michelangelo.
His interpretation is, nevertheless,
probably the most beautiful ever
made, and it is perhaps significant
that it is the only work he signed.

Michelangelo's solution of the
problem posed by the placing of a
full grown man across the knees of
a seated woman is to build up a
pyramid of drapery as a support. At
the same time he takes his treatment
out of the realm of the realistic by
idealizing both figures so that each
represents perfection, bodily and
divine. The criticism that the Virgin
looks too young is thus irrelevant.

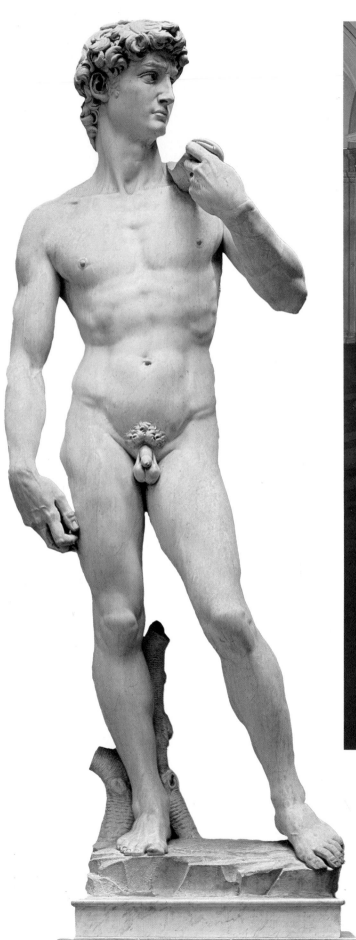

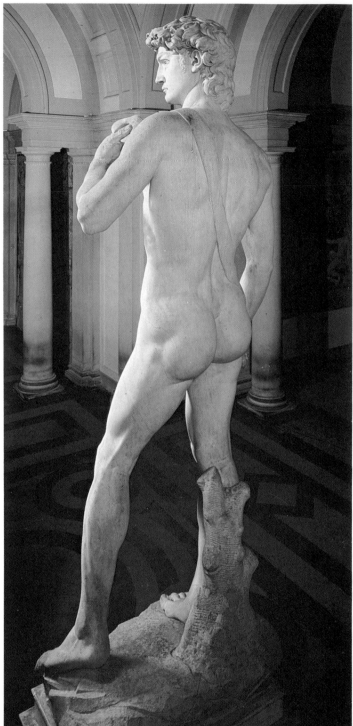

David
1501–4
Marble
410 cm (161½ in) high
Florence: Accademia di Belle Arti

This monumental work was
originally placed in front of the
Palazzo della Signoria (or Palazzo
Vecchio, the town hall of Florence),
but in 1873, in order to protect it
from further damage by the elements,
it was moved to the Accademia.

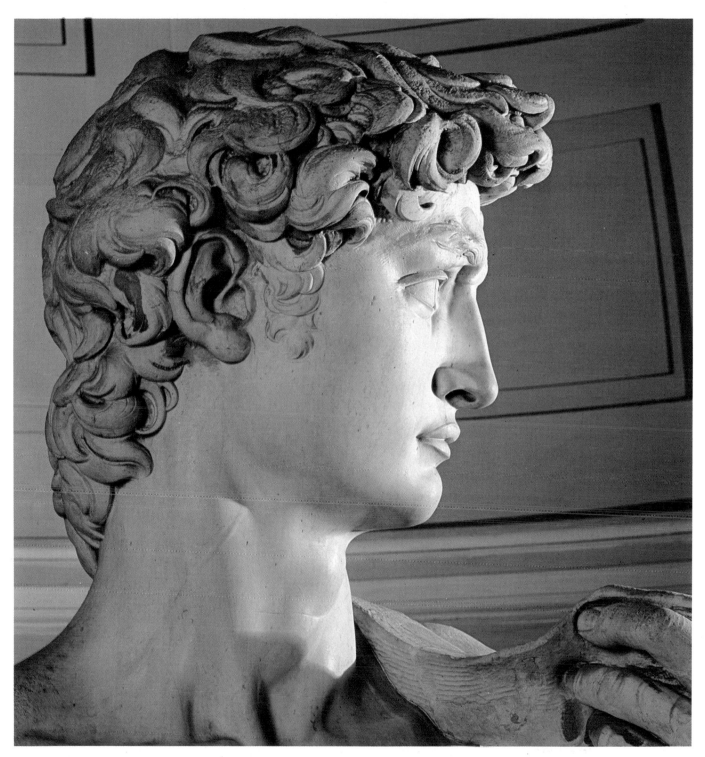

The Old Testament story of the Jewish boy hero David, who slew the Philistine giant Goliath with his sling, symbolizes the victory of intelligence over brute force. It was thus entirely appropriate that the restored Florentine republic should commission Michelangelo to carve this *David*. Unlike his predecessors, Donatello and Verrocchio, who had depicted the victorious hero with the giant's severed head, Michelangelo chose to represent him just before the combat, his brow furrowed with concentration as he looks up towards his towering opponent.

Although the torso is perfectly classical in its treatment of the musculature, the head and hands are much larger in scale than those on ancient statues. These are the proportions of a young man not yet fully grown, but whose potential is already apparent.

Its overwhelming beauty led Vasari to assert: '. . . of a truth whoever has seen this work need not trouble to see any other work executed in sculpture, either in our own or in other times, by no matter what craftsman'.

Like the *Bacchus*, the figure can be appreciated from all angles, the straight right leg acting like a pivot as one walks round the statue.

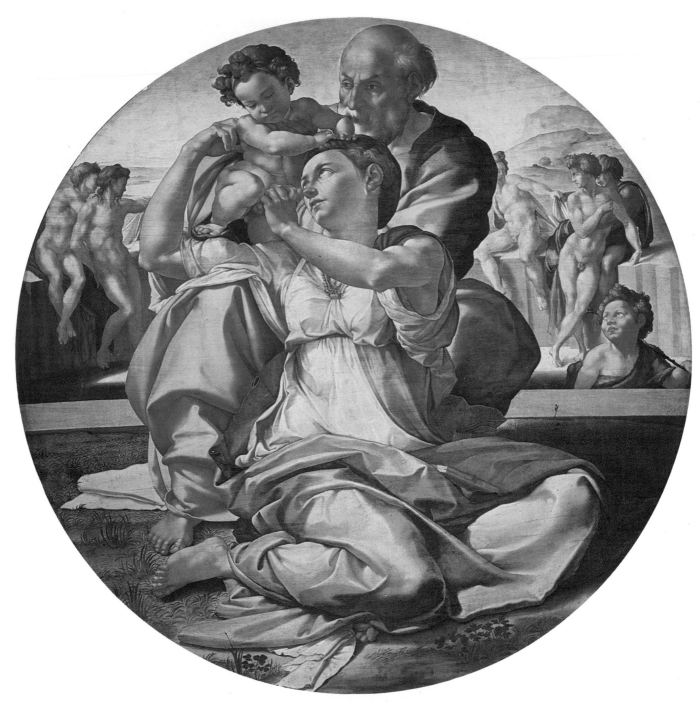

The Doni Tondo
1503–4
Tempera on panel
91 × 80 cm (36 × 31½ in)
Florence: Uffizi

This circular picture (tondo) was painted on the occasion of the marriage of Agnolo Doni and Maddalena Strozzi. It is Michelangelo's first recorded painting. The central group of the Virgin and Child with St Joseph is constructed as a pyramid of interrelated forms which Michelangelo seems to have taken from Leonardo da Vinci who had returned to Florence in 1500. The twist given to the body of the Virgin, who turns to take the Christ child from Joseph, is, however, highly characteristic of Michelangelo.

The most unusual feature of the work is the frieze of nude youths in the background, who may be presumed to represent the pagan world, in which personal relationships are conceived in a spirit of pre-Christian innocence. The two youths on the extreme right embrace, while their companion tries to separate them, watched by the pair on the left. The little boy on the right in the middle distance is St John the Baptist, whose preaching prepared the world for Christ's coming. He links the two zones in the picture, defined by the straight line of wall, behind which stretches a sort of semi-circular amphitheatre from which he gazes up at the Holy Family.

The nudes were soon to reappear on a far larger scale as the 'ignudi' of the Sistine Chapel ceiling.

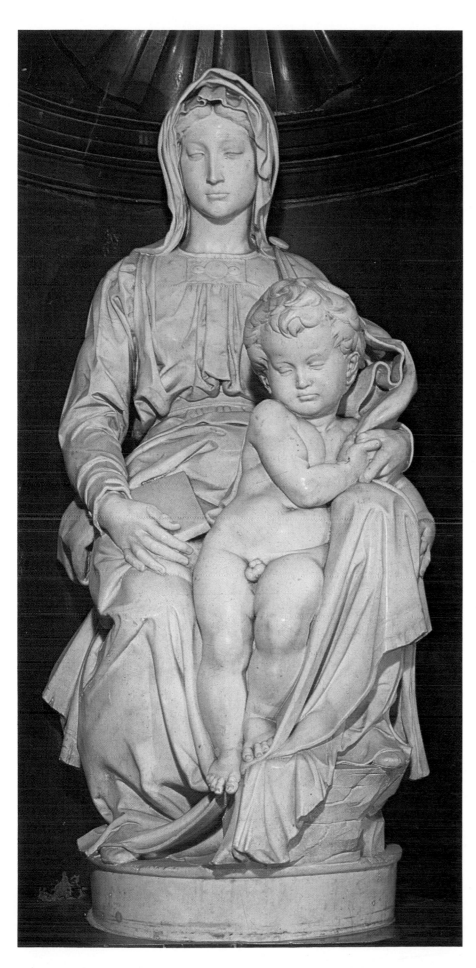

The Bruges Madonna
1503–4
Marble
128 cm (50½ in) high
Bruges: Notre Dame

The precise origin of this commission is unknown, but in December 1503 Michelangelo accepted the first of two payments for the *Madonna* from Alexandre Mouscron, a Flemish cloth merchant, who made a second in October 1504. It was not until the middle of 1506 that Michelangelo, in Rome, arranged with his father in Florence to have the work sent to Viareggio, where it was placed aboard a ship destined for Bruges. It was installed in the church of Notre Dame, where it has remained ever since, except for a period during World War 2.

The head of the Madonna recalls the Rome *Pietà*, with similar treatment of the drapery and facial expression. As a whole, however, the composition is more compact than the earlier work, with the Christ child entirely contained within the confines of the group. The Madonna faces squarely towards the spectator, whereas the Child twists the upper part of His body round to grasp His Mother's hand. His head, however, remains in line with that of the Madonna and both look down in thoughtful sadness, as though aware of Christ's future suffering and death.

The front of the statue is highly finished, but the back, although carved with a bold sweep of heavy drapery, was left unpolished, as it was clearly always intended to be placed in a niche or alcove.

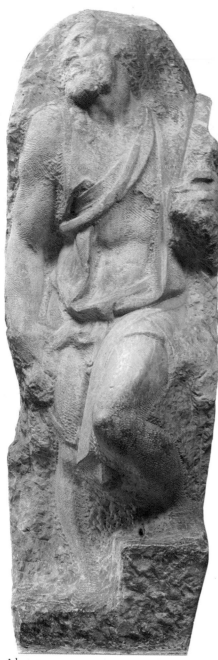

Above
St Matthew
c.1505–6
Marble
271 cm (106½ in) high
Florence: Accademia di Belle Arti

This majestic, if incomplete, figure is
the only one begun of a series of 12
apostles, intended for Florence
Cathedral, that Michelangelo
undertook in April 1503 to complete
at the rate of one a year. He
probably began it before he left
Florence for Rome in March 1505,
and he seems to have resumed work
on it after his precipitate departure
from Rome in April 1506, angered by
the Pope's reluctance to reimburse
him for his expenditure on marble

for the Tomb. It was transferred in
1834 from the Opera del Duomo to
the Accademia, where it is shown
together with the somewhat later
Slaves (see pages 38 and 39).

It has always been seen as a
perfect illustration of Michelangelo's
method of working, as Vasari notes:
'(this) statue, rough as it is, reveals
its full perfection and teaches
sculptors in what manner figures
can be carved out of marble without
their coming out misshapen, so that
it may be possible to go on ever
improving them by removing more of
the marble with judgement and also
to draw back and change some part
according as the necessity may
arise'.

In its present, unfinished state,
the figure gives an impression of
barely contained strength,
anticipating, albeit unintentionally,
the work of a 19th-century sculptor
such as Rodin.

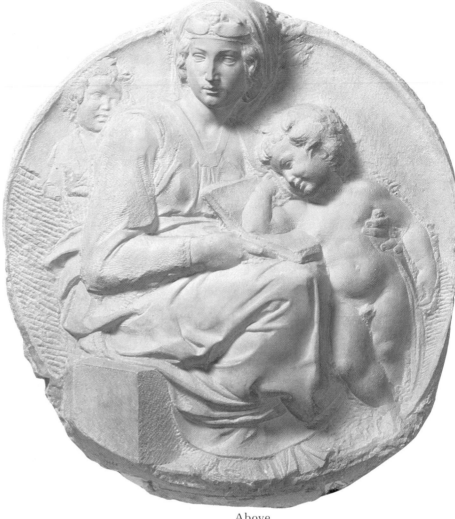

Above
The Pitti Tondo
1504–5
Marble
82 cm (32¼ in) diameter
Florence: Museo Nazionale (Bargello)

According to Vasari, this was begun
for Bartolommeo Pitti, whose son
gave it to a member of the
Guicciardini family, from whom it
was acquired in 1823 for the Bargello.

Like the *Taddei tondo*, it depicts
the Holy Family with St John the
Baptist but, whereas in that work
Michelangelo brilliantly exploits the
constricting circular form, here he
seems to have become impatient
with it so that the Madonna's head
projects beyond the frame. It is the
most finished part and the face is of
a completely different character from
the *Pietà* or the *Bruges Madonna*,
having a more rounded mature form
that looks forward to the *Delphic
Sibyl* on the Sistine Chapel ceiling.
The expression, too, seems more
philosophical, and less tender, in
accordance with the monumental
quality of what is, surprisingly, the
smallest of the three tondi.

No conclusive explanation has
been offered as to why the work

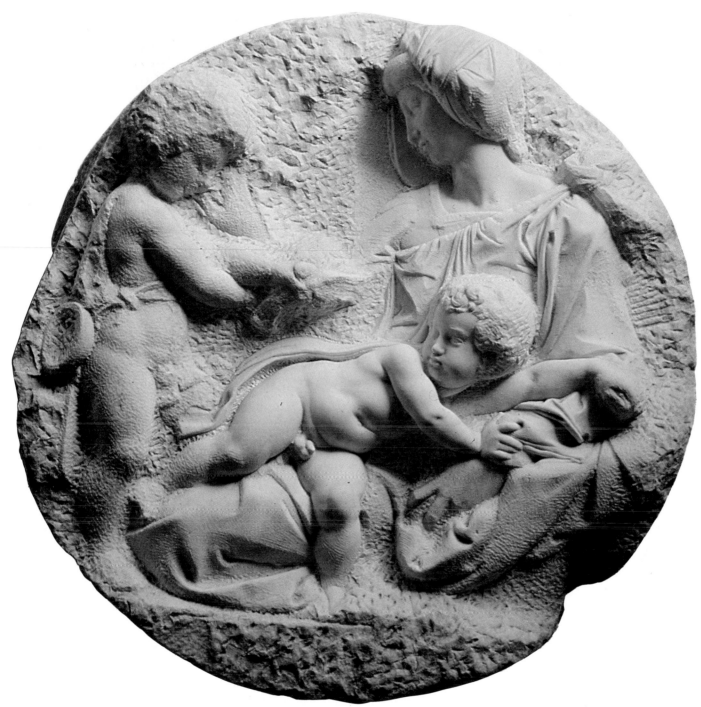

was left unfinished, although the arrival of Pope Julius II in Bologna, where Michelangelo was summoned to appear before him in November 1506, has been suggested.

Above
The Taddei Tondo
1504–5
Marble
109 cm (42$\frac{7}{8}$ in) diameter
London: Royal Academy

This unfinished work was made for the Florentine Taddeo Taddei, in whose family it remained until the 19th century, when it was acquired in Rome by Sir George Beaumont, who presented it to the Royal Academy in London, where it is on permanent public view.

It shows the Madonna and Child, with the infant St John who is offering a goldfinch to Jesus, from which he leans away, gazing back at it in fear. This bird is a symbol of Christ's suffering and death on the cross and is based on a tradition that it feeds on thorns, thus prefiguring the crown of thorns placed on Christ's head before the crucifixion. The pose of the Christ child (for which there are two drawings in the British Museum) creates a diagonal line to which everything else in the composition relates. This is precisely echoed by the line of the Madonna's tunic and the angle of her head as she gazes impassively at St John. It is not clear how the tondo would have been completed though it has been suggested that a landscape background would have been indicated, as the presence of the goldfinch in an interior would be unlikely. The dating 1504–5 is usually accepted although one slightly earlier (1500–2) has also been proposed.

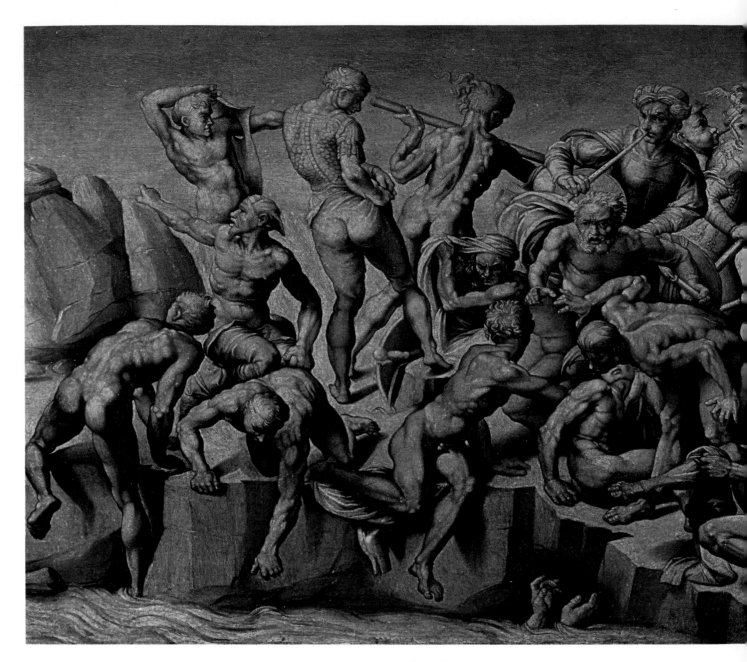

Aristotile da Sangallo (1481–1551)
The Battle of Cascina
(Also known as **The Cartoon of Pisa**)
c. 1542
Oil on panel
76 × 129 cm (30 × 50¾ in)
Norfolk: Holkham Hall, Viscount Coke

This copy of the central section of Michelangelo's cartoon (1504–5) for his fresco in the Palazzo della Signoria in Florence is the most important surviving indication of the artist's total conception. Some of his own drawings exist, but these are sketchy or of individual figures only.

The incident that Michelangelo chose as his main subject was not the actual battle, but one that took place the day before, when the Florentine soldiers, overcome by the heat, stripped to bathe in the River Arno. One of their number, seeing how unprepared they would be in the event of an attack by their enemies, the Pisans, sounded a false alarm, upon which the soldiers clambered out of the water and struggled into their clothes. It would be difficult to imagine a more perfect opportunity for depicting the nude male in violent action and Michelangelo exploits it to the full. That the subject matter was merely a pretext for creating a repertory of male nudes was clearly appreciated by his contemporaries, who used it virtually as an art school. Leonardo foresaw the danger that lesser painters would copy the figures and reuse them out of context, which is precisely what happened.

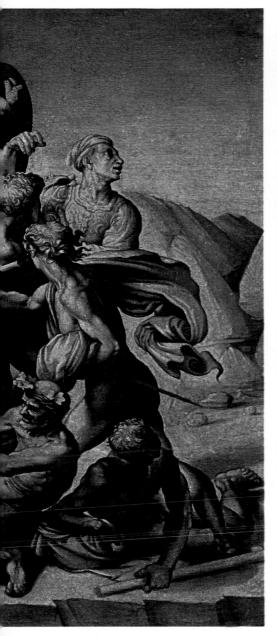

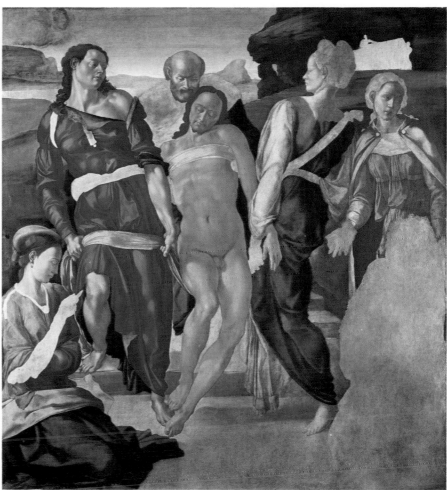

Above
The Entombment
Begun 1506
Oil on panel
161 × 149 cm (63⅔ × 58⅔ in)
London: National Gallery

Although not accepted by all writers
as a Michelangelo, it is catalogued
as by him in Cecil Gould's *The
Sixteenth-century Italian Schools*
(National Gallery, London, 1975) and
is described most recently (by Linda
Murray, 1980) as presenting
'characteristics which make it very
difficult to assign to any other
artist'. It is recorded in the Farnese
collection in Rome by 1693 and later
in the collection of Cardinal Fesch. It
was eventually acquired by the
British painter, Robert Macpherson,
from whom it was purchased in
1868. It is unfinished.
    The subject is the moment before
the dead Christ was placed in the
tomb. The identification of most of
the figures presents difficulties: for
example, the bearer on the left,
usually called St John, is identified
by Gould as Nicodemus. There is,
however, general agreement that the
pose of this striking figure is derived
from one of the most famous statues
of antiquity, the *Laocoön*, whose
rediscovery on 14 January 1506 in
Rome was actually witnessed by
Michelangelo.
    Gould suggests that the work was
brought to its present state in two
stages, the first between 14 January
and 17 April 1506, while
Michelangelo was in Rome awaiting
delivery of marble from Carrara, and
the second some five or six years
later. It may have been intended to
adorn the interior of the chamber
which was a feature of the first
project for the Tomb of Julius II.

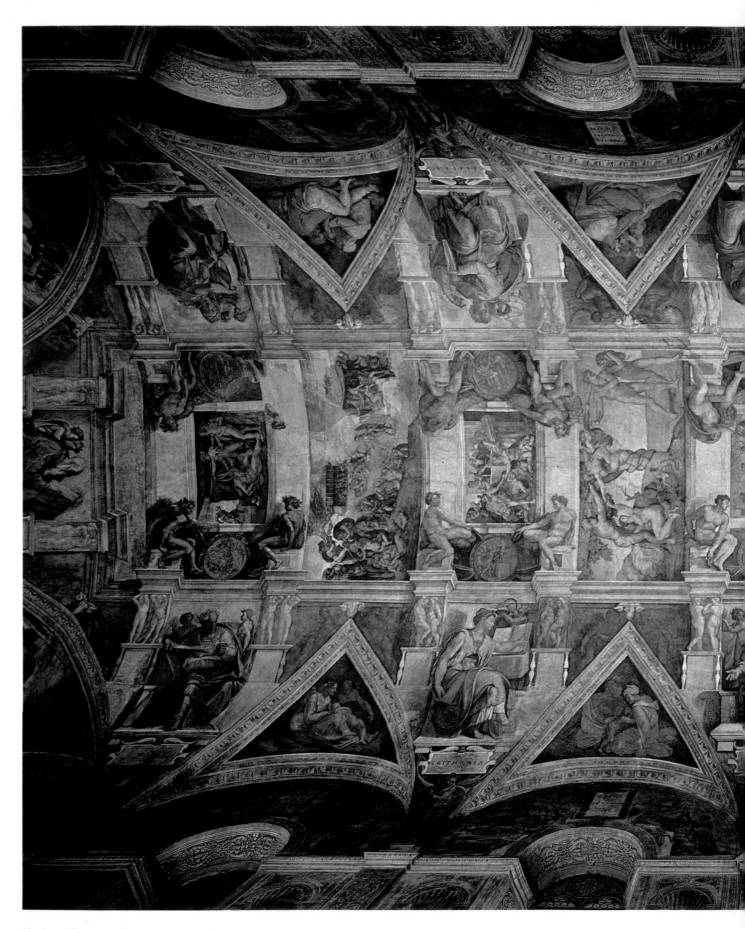

Sistine Chapel ceiling

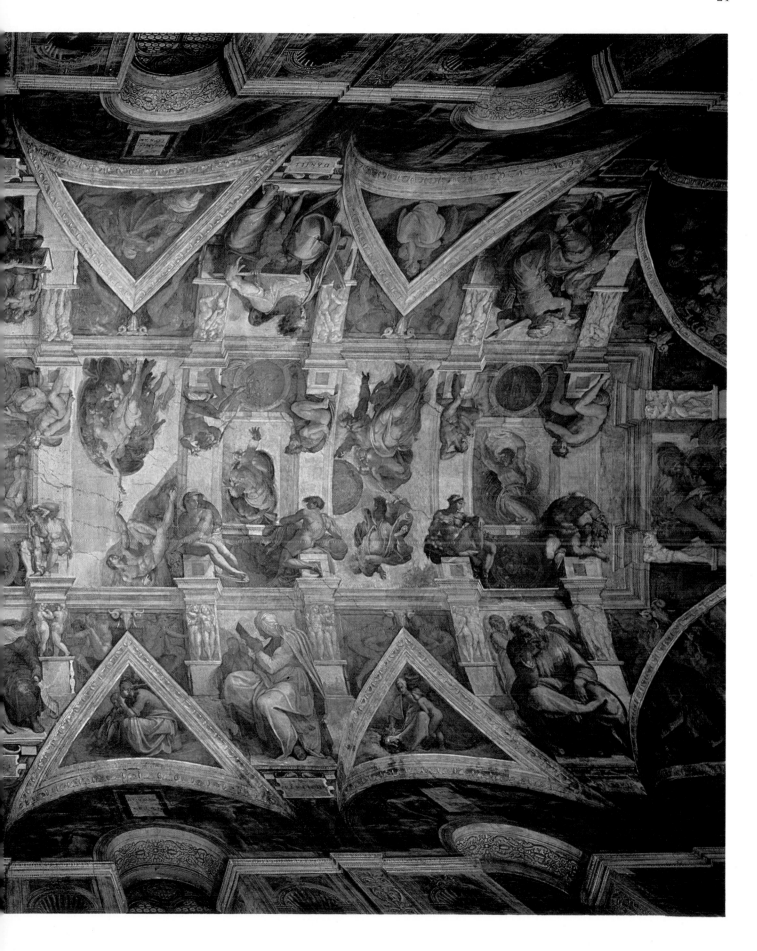

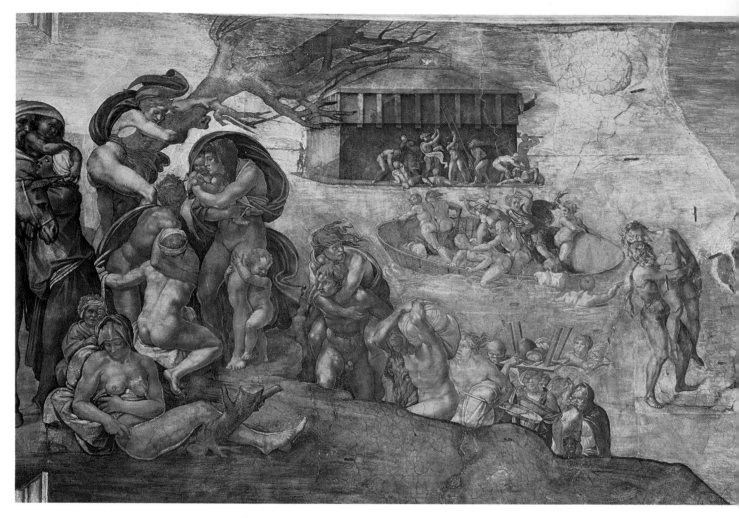

Previous pages
Sistine Chapel ceiling
1508–12
Fresco
13 × 40 metres (42 ft 8 in × 132 ft)
approx
Rome: Vatican

Taking its name from Pope Sixtus
IV, who had it built, the Sistine
Chapel was intended as a setting for
important papal ceremonies,
including the Conclave. This is the
assembly of cardinals which meets
on the death of a pope to elect his
successor.

The ceiling was originally painted
in dark blue, patterned with gold
stars. When Pope Julius II
commissioned Michelangelo to
redecorate it, he suggested the 12
Apostles as the subject. What
Michelangelo executed was nothing
less than the story of the Creation of
the World.

*Details from the Sistine Chapel
ceiling*

Above
The Deluge

Although this is the penultimate
scene in the story of the Creation
depicted on the central section of
the ceiling in nine episodes, it was
the first to be completed, before June
1509, together with the *Sacrifice of
Noah* and the *Drunkenness of Noah*.

Most depictions of the Flood
include the ark constructed at God's
command by Noah, and this is no
exception, although it occupies a
relatively minor place in the
background. The most prominent
figures are of the nude or partly
nude figures struggling to escape the
rising waters and several of them
clearly derive from the *Battle of
Cascina* cartoon. Some are carrying
pathetic remnants of their household
possessions, others are repulsed by
the occupants from an already
dangerously overloaded boat, and an
old man stands in silent grief
bearing the dead body of his son.

From below, all this detail is

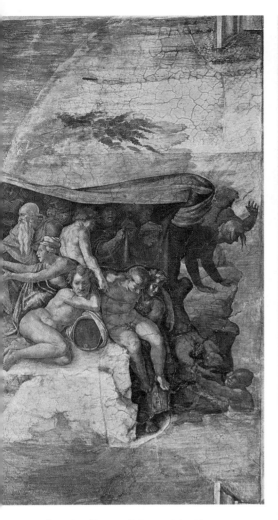

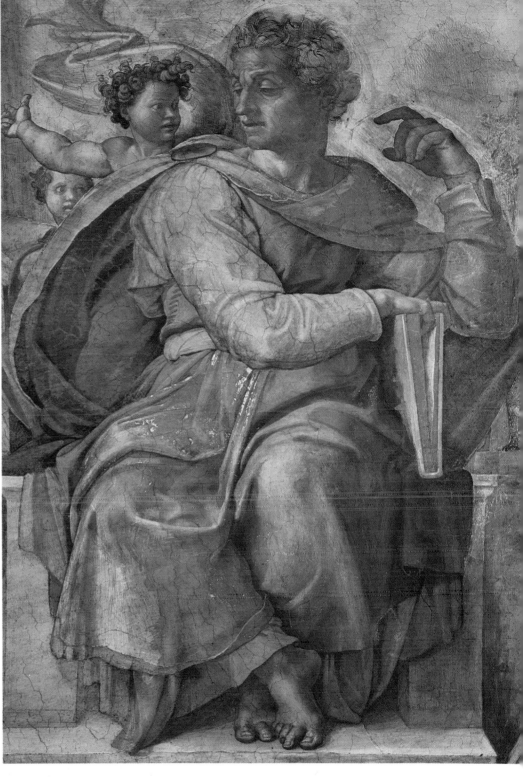

barely discernible and in the flanking, shorter panels, the figures are much larger in scale. This half of the ceiling, which originally covered the part of the chapel open to the public, also includes the *Temptation and Expulsion* (of Adam and Eve) and the *Creation of Eve* which, together with the flanking figures, were finished by August 1510.

Right
The Prophet Isaiah

The pendentives (triangular extensions of the central area of the vault) are occupied alternately by Old Testament Prophets and their pagan equivalents, the sibyls or prophetesses.

Of the seven prophets depicted, Isaiah is one of the most important, foretelling man's redemption through the life and death of Christ. He is placed below the *Sacrifice of Noah*, listening attentively to the words of prophecy relayed to him by the infant genius beside him. Opposite him sits the Erythraean Sibyl, who is credited with having foretold the Last Judgement.

The other prophets portrayed are Jeremiah, Daniel and Ezekiel, who are considered major, together with three lesser figures, Zechariah, Joel and Jonah. Jonah, nevertheless, occupies a crucial position, in the pendentive above the high altar. This is because he is taken to prefigure Christ's burial and Resurrection, having spent three days in the belly of the whale, just as Christ was to spend three days in the tomb.

In addition to their literal virtues as prophets, it has been suggested that each one represents a gift of the Holy Spirit, so that he has a symbolic significance as well. Isaiah would thus be equated with Counsel.

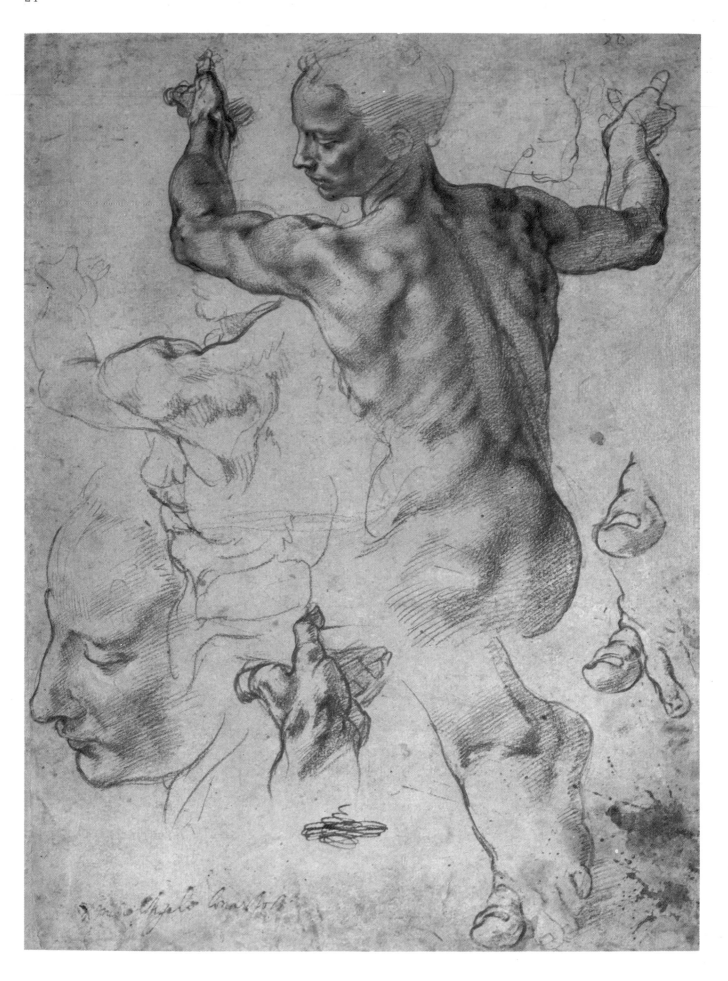

The Libyan Sibyl

This magnificent figure, among the
last to be painted (*c*.1511), is placed
below the first scene of the Creation,
the *Separation of Light from
Darkness*, and is balanced on the
opposite side by the prophet
Jeremiah.

The deliberately contorted pose
presents Michelangelo with an
anatomical challenge to which he
responds brilliantly, as can be seen
(left) from the sheet of studies for
the figure in the Metropolitan
Museum, New York (red chalk,
29×21.5 cm/$11\frac{3}{8} \times 8\frac{1}{2}$ in). The
musculature of the back makes it at
once apparent that the model was
male, and in fact there is no reason
to suppose that Michelangelo ever
drew from the nude female model.
The other studies, for the sibyl's
profile, left hand and left foot, show
the scrupulous care Michelangelo
took to work out every detail of each
figure. This was essential, bearing in
mind the technique which he
employed, known as 'buon fresco',
where the colour is applied to the
plaster while it is still wet, which
does not allow for any mistakes.

As well as fulfilling her prophetic
role, the Libyan Sibyl may be seen
as the personification of energetic
young womanhood.

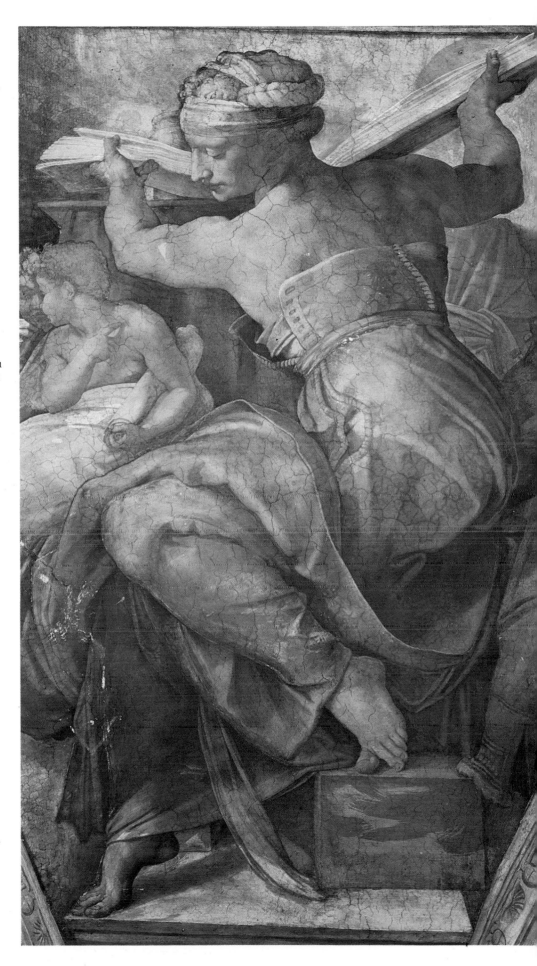

Right
The Creation of Adam

Work on the ceiling had stopped in August 1510, when Michelangelo had reached the original line of the screen separating the public and private halves of the chapel. It has since been moved, but the division can still be seen in the exquisite cosmati pavement. There seems to be some doubt as to the exact relationship of the *Creation of Eve* to this line, since Howard Hibbard places it on the pope's side and Linda Murray on the public's.

Be that as it may, after its completion there was an interval caused by the absence of the Pope on a military campaign against his rebellious subjects in Emilia and the consequent lack of funds to take down and re-erect the special scaffolding that Michelangelo had designed.

The first panel of the second half, the *Creation of Adam*, is one of the most successful of the whole undertaking, and possibly the artist's best-known image. The figure of Adam, reclining with natural elegance that can only be described as god-like, awaits the touch that will bestow on him the supreme gift of life. God the Father, whose cloak billows out to reveal the souls of the as yet unborn, including Eve, descends from the skies and stretches out his hand towards the first man. That their fingers just do not touch can only be described as the inspiration of genius.

A fine study (below right) for Adam in the British Museum (red chalk, 19.3 × 25.9 cm/7⅝ × 10¼ in) again shows Michelangelo's attention to anatomical detail with each muscle accurately indicated.

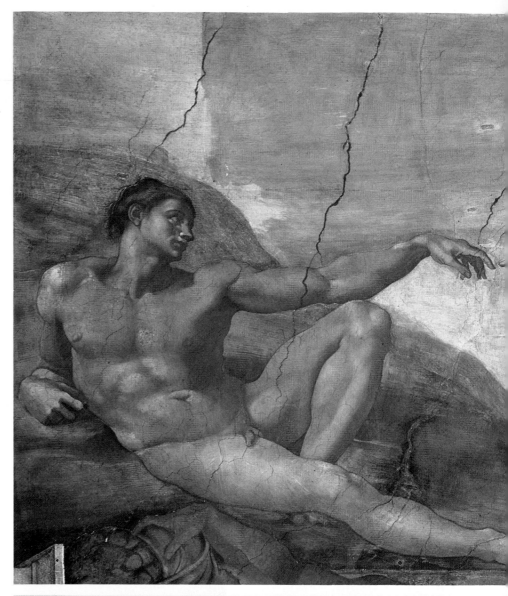

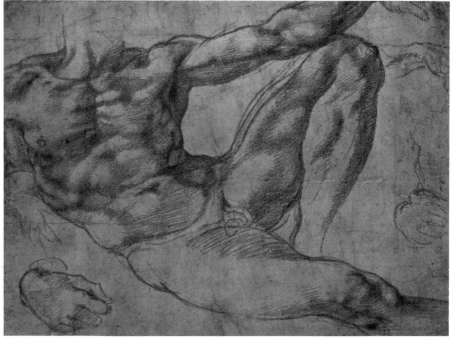

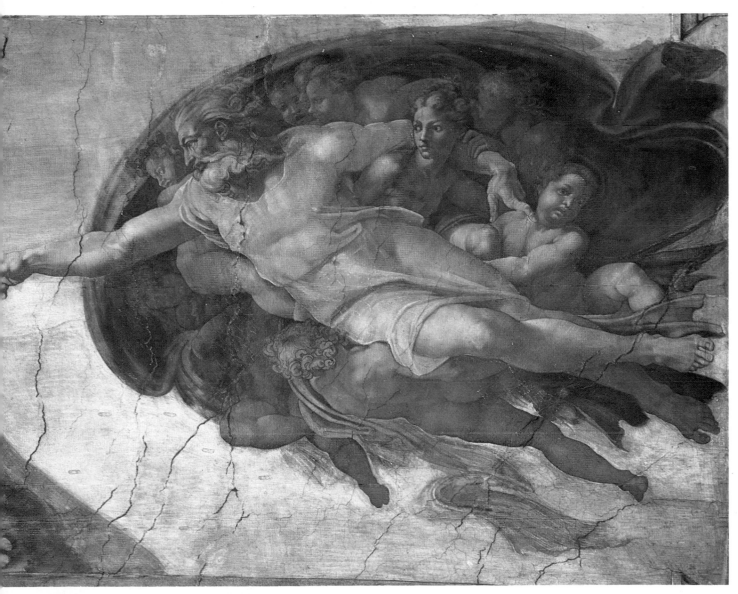

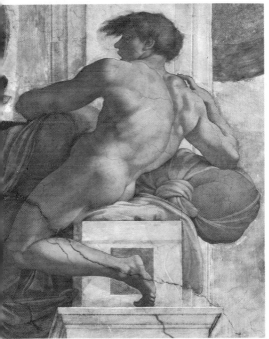

Left
An Ignudo

This one is seated at the corner of the third panel from the end opposite the high altar, which depicts the *Separation of Land from Water*, rightly considered as one of the most forceful of the series, dominated as it is by the huge figure of God who appears to be descending from the heavens upon the spectator.

The *ignudi* have always presented problems to scholars trying to interpret the complex imagery of the ceiling. Are they angels, without wings? Are they athletes? If so, why are they included? Their apparent function is to act as supporters for the fictive bronze medallions at either end of each of the shorter panels. In addition, some of them bear garlands of oak leaves and acorns, the emblem of the Della Rovere family of Pope Julius II.

The earlier pairs are more or less mirror images of each other but, in the second half of the ceiling, Michelangelo gives his imagination a freer rain and each one is individualized. This one, open-mouthed, wild-eyed and with his hair blown forward as if by an unearthly wind, seems to be an eye-witness of the tremendous event taking place above him and is thus acting as a link not only between the central area of the ceiling and the pendentives, peopled by the prophets and sibyls, but also with the human spectators far below.

Strivings in Stone

The Sistine Chapel ceiling is described by Vasari as 'the lamp of our art' and he relates how, 'when the work was thrown open, the whole world could be heard running up to see it'. The Pope, delighting in Michelangelo's achievement as much as evidence of his own discerning patronage as for the ceiling itself, lavished money and presents upon its creator. However, Michelangelo was not allowed long to recover from the strain and exhaustion produced by years of working flat on his back. This had, in Vasari's words, 'so impaired his sight that for a time which was not less than several months, he was not able to read letters or look at drawings save with his head backwards'.

Pope Julius's thoughts immediately returned to the interrupted project for his tomb, now a matter of greater urgency since he sensed his approaching death, which in fact took place a few months later, on 21 February 1513. He had already placed upon two cardinals, Lorenzo Pucci and Leonardo Grosso della Rovere, the responsibility for overseeing its completion after his death, and it was with them that Michelangelo negotiated a new contract dated 6 May 1513. The concept of a free-standing monument was abandoned, but the new design, although related to a wall, was to project from it by almost twice its own width, and was to be surmounted by a high, arched feature, like a small chapel. The number of figures was slightly reduced, from 40 to 35, but some of them, including the effigy of the Pope, were to be twice life size.

In the event, Michelangelo completed only three figures of which just one, the *Moses*, found a place on the Pope's tomb in San Pietro in Vincoli, while the two *Slaves* entered the French royal collection and are now in the Louvre.

Meanwhile, in Florence, the Medici family had been dramatically restored to power thanks to the support of a papal army headed by Cardinal Giovanni de' Medici, who shortly afterwards became Pope as Leo X. Writing from Rome to his brother Buonarroti in Florence on 18 September 1512, Michelangelo advises circumspection: '. . . live peacefully, and do not become friendly nor intimate with anyone, except God. Do not speak well nor evil of anybody, for one never knows how things end up; just mind your own business.'

At first the new Pope had no work for Michelangelo, even though, as a son of Lorenzo the Magnificent, he had known him since childhood, but towards the end of 1515 Leo seems to have conceived the notion of commissioning a façade for the family church of San Lorenzo in Florence. Such a prestigious undertaking in his native city would inevitably have appealed to Michelangelo, although Vasari insists that he was unwilling to shoulder the responsibility, being committed to the completion of Julius II's Tomb, for which he signed a third contract in July 1516. This time the commission was for a version greatly reduced in size and with fewer figures, to be carried out within nine years in whatever location he should choose. This left Michelangelo free to live in Florence, where he could also work on the San Lorenzo façade, for which he made first a clay and then a wooden model.

The contract for the façade was eventually made with Leo in January 1518 but the Pope insisted on using marble from new quarries in Florentine territory, which involved not only building an access road before quarrying could get under way, but also aroused the resentment of the Carrara marble workers who revenged themselves by fomenting a

Moses
c. 1515
Marble
235 cm (92½ in) high
Rome: San Pietro in Vincoli

Although originally intended to be paired with a St Paul, the *Moses* occupies the central bay of the lowest section of the Tomb of Pope Julius II, an unfortunate position since it was originally intended to be seen from below, and carved with this in mind.

In spite of this, its impact is overwhelming and Vasari's story that the Jews of Rome flocked to pay their respects to it every sabbath, in spite of the commandment forbidding 'graven images', is easily credible.

Moses is depicted with the tablets of the law which he had received on Mount Sinai, and with the horns on his head which derive from a mistranslation of the Hebrew word for 'rays' indicating a halo. His face expresses the supreme authority which his role as God's messenger to the Israelites has given him, rather than anger, and the notion that he is rebuking his people for worshipping the golden calf is a misinterpretation of this tremendous work.

Apart from one or two minor areas, the statue is completely finished. The deeply cut coils of the majestic beard, the veins on his powerful left arm and the mass of folded drapery above his right knee make this a masterpiece of technique as well as of invention.

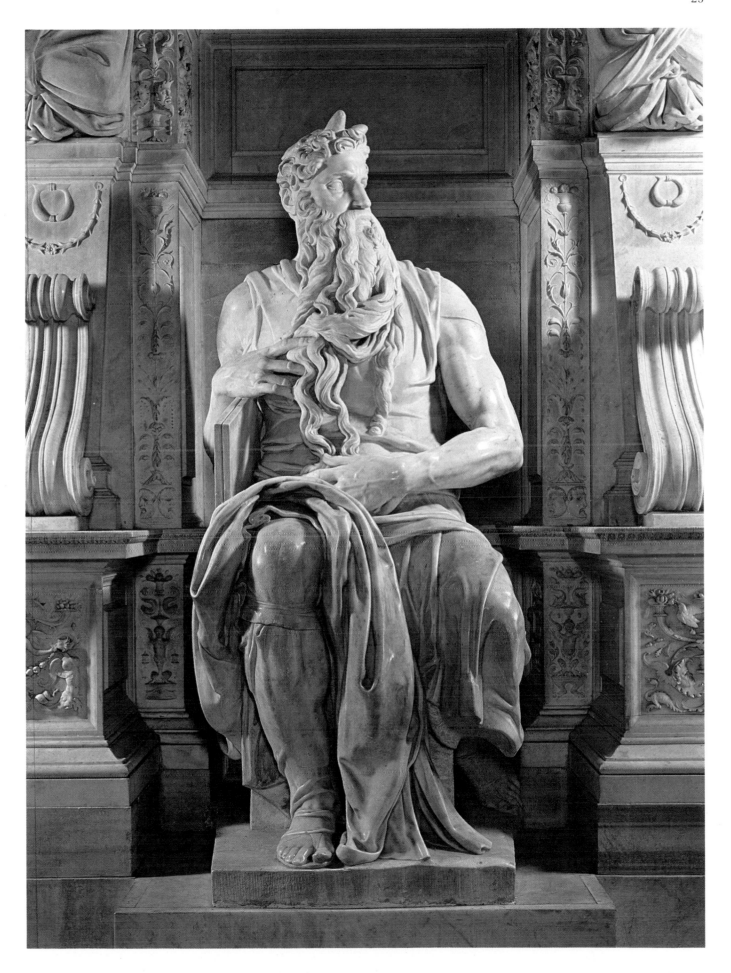

strike of bargemen. The resultant saga of illness, accident and intrigue continued until, at the beginning of 1520, the Pope himself dealt Michelangelo a final humiliating blow by suddenly cancelling the contract. The wooden model which still survives in the Casa Buonarroti in Florence shows how it would have looked, with two main storeys articulated by classical columns (below) and pilasters (above), crowned by a triangular pediment above the central bay.

A similar formula was employed for the interior of a structure that Michelangelo actually built at San Lorenzo, the New Sacristy, commissioned by Cardinal Giulio de' Medici (later Pope Clement VII) as a resting place for the bodies of four members of the family, including the last in the direct line from 'old' Cosimo, the founder of the dynasty. Work seems to have started on this even before the abandonment of the façade project and by the end of April 1521 the walls had reached cornice level. At the death of Leo X, a Dutchman briefly became Pope as Adrian VI and the thoroughly dissatisfied executors of Julius II's will petitioned him to put pressure on Michelangelo to complete the Tomb, threatening to bring a lawsuit. By this time (November 1523) another Medici occupied the papal throne and Clement was naturally more concerned with the family chapel in San Lorenzo, together with the simultaneous project for a library to house Lorenzo the Magnificent's collection of manuscripts.

At the beginning of 1524 the structure of the Medici Chapel (as the New Sacristy is usually called) was complete and by April Michelangelo had begun carving the figures, four of which were almost finished in just under a year. However, politics once more intervened to deflect Michelangelo from his work, and the quarrel between the Pope and the Holy Roman Emperor, Charles V, led to yet another invasion of the Italian peninsula. This culminated in the Sack of Rome in May 1527 by the Imperial troops and the imprisonment of the Pope in Castel Sant'Angelo. The Medici were again expelled from Florence and Michelangelo was put in charge of the fortifications of the city, which was threatened by the combined armies of Pope and Emperor. Both were now reconciled and equally opposed to the Florentine Republic, which capitulated on 12 August 1530. Thanks to one of the canons of San Lorenzo, Michelangelo was able to hide from the wrath of the triumphant papal governor who had ordered his assassination, and for whom, after having been pardoned by the Pope, he began the unfinished *David-Apollo*, now in the Bargello, Florence. During the absence of the Medici he had returned to the project that was to hang over him for 40 years, the Tomb. He roughed out the four figures of slaves which are now in the Accademia in Florence and which more than any of Michelangelo's works demonstrate his manner of working by liberating the figure which he saw as imprisoned in the stone. A fourth contract for a simplified wall tomb, to be erected in San Pietro in Vincoli, was signed in April 1532, after further protracted negotiations. However, at the same time the Pope insisted that, apart from completing the Tomb, Michelangelo was to work only for him, on pain of excommunication.

By the middle of 1532 Michelangelo was preparing to divide his time between Florence and Rome, spending most of it in his native city, but two events persuaded him to change his mind: the violent and probably insane Alessandro de' Medici was made Duke of Tuscany, and Michelangelo developed a deep personal relationship with a young Roman nobleman, Tommaso de' Cavalieri. Michelangelo addressed letters and sonnets to him that, despite their extravagant phraseology and conventional imagery, speak of an overwhelming emotional, rather than physical, experience. Indeed, Ascanio Condivi, a pupil of Michelangelo, who published in 1553 what is virtually the artist's autobiography, makes a particular point of emphasizing Michelangelo's abhorrence of anything 'lewd and shameful' in such a relationship. That he was indifferent to the female body is obvious from his art and indeed his only close female friend, Vittoria Colonna, Marchesa di Pescara, whom he probably met in 1538, was a pious intellectual who presumably relished his basically asexual devotion.

Right
The Dying Slave
1513–6
Marble
229 cm (90$\frac{1}{8}$ in) high

Far right
The Rebellious Slave
1513–6
Marble
215 cm (84$\frac{5}{8}$ in) high
Paris: Musée du Louvre

Originally intended for the tomb of Julius II, these *Slaves*, or more correctly *Captives*, would have been placed against the supports of the main structure, at ground floor level. In the first project there were to have been 16 of them, but by 1532 their number had been reduced to four, and, in the event, Michelangelo discarded them altogether. He gave them as a gesture of thanks to his friend Roberto Strozzi for the care that he had received in his house. Strozzi was then (1546) living in exile at Lyon and he gave them to the French King, Francis I, who in turn bestowed them on the Connétable de Montmorency, who installed them on the face of his country house, the Château d'Écouen. In the 17th century they passed into the hands of Cardinal Richelieu and in 1794 they were acquired by the revolutionary government for the French nation.

The *Dying Slave* is not dying, but has merely ceased to struggle against the bonds that hold him. His body is lovingly sculpted, although the musculature is less defined than in the *David*, which is in any case a body in tension, whereas the *Slave* is languid to the point of passivity. The curious unfinished block at the back of the statue appears to represent an ape or a monkey, for which numberless explanations have been offered, usually derived from the concept of 'Art as the ape of Nature'. However, it is not even certain that this supporting block would have remained once the statue had been placed in position, and this curious little figure may be a rare instance of Michelangelo's sardonic sense of humour.

The *Rebellious Slave* is, by contrast, struggling against the constriction of his bonds, and it is difficult not to believe that the two figures must have been intended in some way to balance each other. It has been suggested that this slave was intended as a corner figure on the tomb, with the more directly frontal *Dying Slave* next to it.

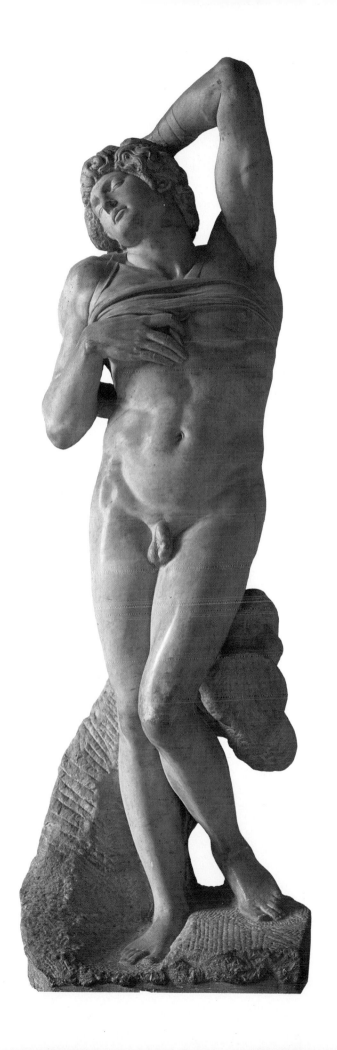
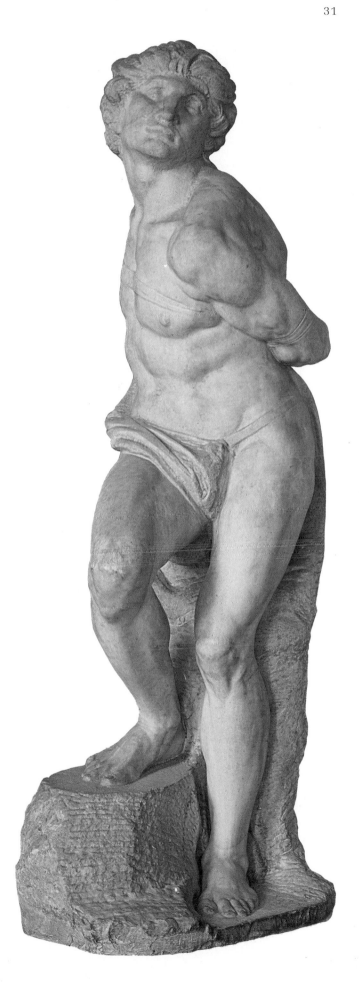

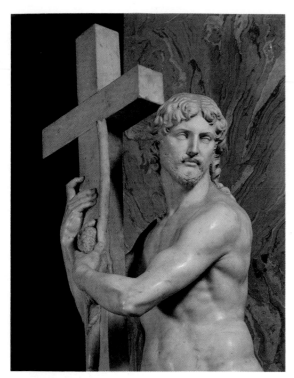

Above
The Risen Christ (detail)
1519–20
Marble
205 cm (80¾ in) high
Rome: Santa Maria sopra Minerva

Commissioned in 1514 by three
Roman patrons, Bernardo Cencio,
Maria Scapucci and Metello Vari
Porcari, the first version of this
statue developed a disfiguring black
vein while Michelangelo was carving
the face. Although Porcari accepted
it in its unfinished state, he insisted
on a second version. This was begun
in Florence in 1519 and sent two
years later to Rome, where
Michelangelo's pupil, Pietro Urbano,
gave it some generally unsatisfactory
final touches, particularly to the
face.

Christ stands holding some of the
symbols of his cruel death, the cross
itself, the rope with which he was
beaten, the sponge which a
bystander soaked in vinegar and the
long reed which he used to raise it
to the dying Christ's parched lips.

A nude Christ was perfectly
acceptable during the High
Renaissance, but in the 17th century
a hideous gilt metal drapery was
attached to the figure thus
concealing the lower part of the
finely sculpted abdomen.
Fortunately, an exquisite drawing
for this part exists, in the collection
of Brinsley Ford, London.

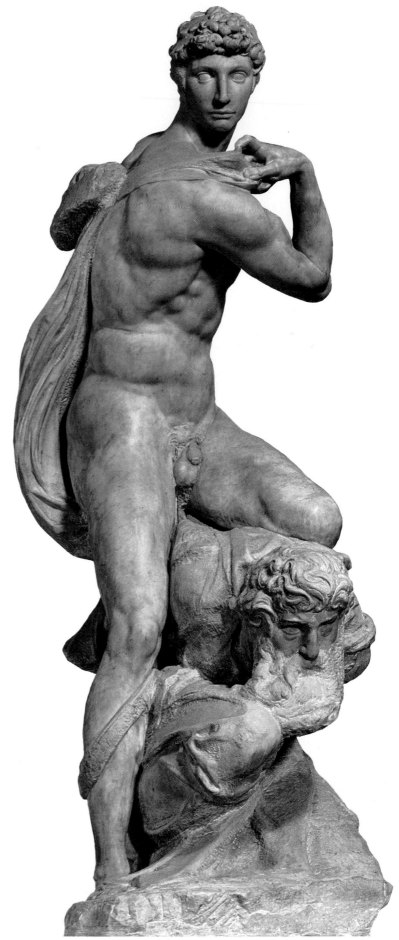

Left
Victory
Block cut *c.*1516,
probably carved 1527–30
Marble
261 cm (102¾ in) high
Florence: Palazzo Vecchio

Originally intended to adorn the
tomb of Julius II, this figure seems to
have been blocked out, possibly
even as early as 1505–6, although it
was not brought to its present state
until very much later. In any case, it
was not destined to adorn the tomb,
but remained in the artist's
possession and was inherited by his
nephew, who presented it to the
Grand Duke Cosimo de' Medici. In
1565 it was given a place of honour
in the huge Salone dei Cinquecento
(as the council chamber of the
republic was renamed) which was
decorated by Vasari and his
assistants with paintings glorifying
the Medici. It remained there for 300
years but, after being removed to
various locations in Florence, it
returned to its original site in 1980
for the exhibition *Firenze e la
Toscana dei Medici nell' Europa del
Cinquecento*.

The meaning of the group has
never been satisfactorily explained,
since the precise nature of the
victory celebrated is not clear. Its
interpretation as the victory of
Florence over Siena is a late 16th
century one, made to link it up with
the decorative scheme of the hall.
The idea that the youth could
represent Tommaso de' Cavalieri and
the crushed old man Michelangelo
himself has been considered, but it
is difficult to reconcile such a notion
with the work's original destination.
It would also imply a final dating of
not earlier than 1532, when he met
Cavalieri.

Below
The Medici Chapel
1520–34
Florence: San Lorenzo

The architectural design of the New
Sacristy (usually known as the
Medici Chapel) is based upon that
by Filippo Brunelleschi for the Old
Sacristy, but there are significant
modifications, such as the insertion
of a second storey and a completely
novel use of the classical orders.

These 'orders of architecture', based
on different types of classical
column and their associated
features, originated in ancient
Greece, where they were employed
in the construction of temples and
other public buildings. The Romans
adopted them, made them more
elaborate and codified their use. The
writer responsible, Vitruvius, was
regarded by the architects of the
Renaissance as a supreme authority
and, although his rules might be
variously interpreted, their essential
validity was not questioned.

Michelangelo, while perfectly
familiar with the rules, deliberately
breaks them, producing architecture
not only of great originality, but of
extraordinary power. Vasari
mentions this approvingly, adding
that 'the craftsmen owe him an
infinite and everlasting obligation,
he having broken the bonds and
chains by reason of which they had
always followed a beaten path in the
execution of their works'.

The actual construction of the
building proceeded in two stages,
1520–1 and 1523–4, when the
coffered dome, modelled on the
Pantheon in Rome, was completed.

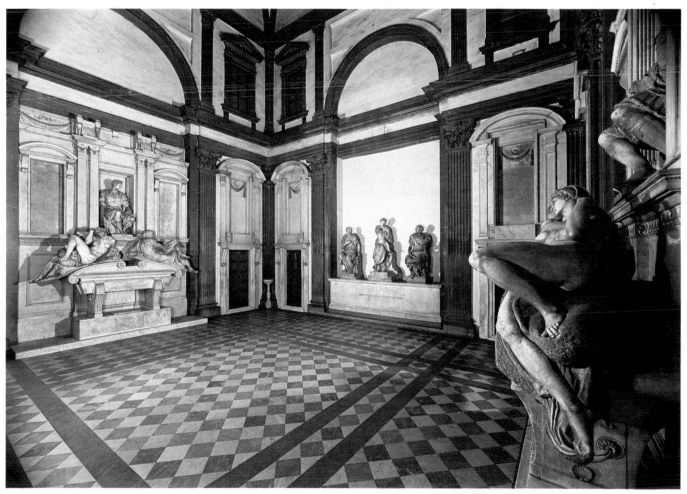

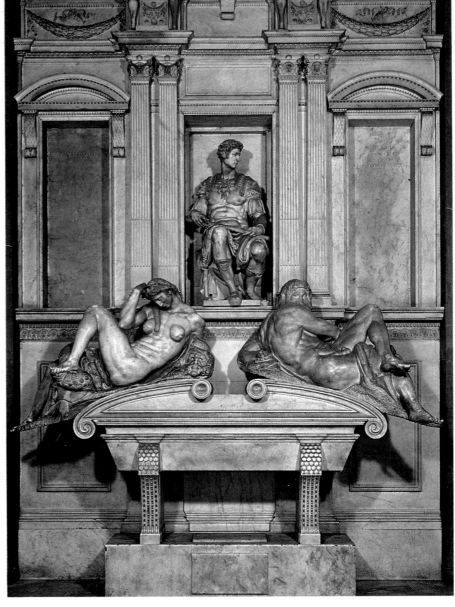

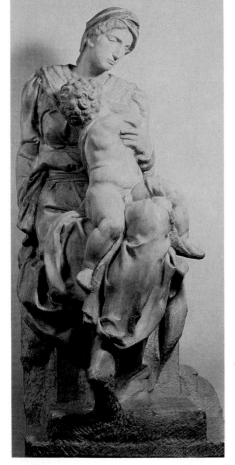

Left
The Medici Madonna
Begun 1521
Marble
253 cm (99½ in) high
Florence: San Lorenzo

On the wall opposite the altar of the Medici Chapel Michelangelo had planned a double tomb for his first patron, Lorenzo the Magnificent, and his brother Giuliano, with, in the centre above them, a statue of the Madonna. Only this last was ever begun by him, as the flanking statues of Saints Cosmas and Damian (patrons of the Medici family) were executed by the assistants who supervised the arrangement of the chapel after Michelangelo's departure in 1534.

The *Medici Madonna* is Michelangelo's last treatment of the subject, but in it he chooses the same aspect that he had selected for his first, that of the Christ child at His mother's breast. Similarly, he shows neither His face nor her breast. Her face, on the contrary, is rendered with exquisite delicacy, in spite of its unpolished state, and the features have a haunted, mysterious quality that seems to convey a sort of reproachful resignation.

Left
The Tomb of Giuliano de' Medici
c. 1531–3
Florence: San Lorenzo

Giuliano de' Medici, Duke of Nemours through his marriage to a princess of the House of Savoy, had died in 1516 at the age of 38, the last in the direct Medici line.

The architectural setting is identical for his tomb and Lorenzo's on the opposite side of the chapel. It comprises a panelled base, against which the sarcophagus or tomb stands, its double scrolled lid supporting two reclining figures. The upper area is divided by pairs of narrow pilasters (flat columns) into three bays, each containing a shallow niche like a blind window. The outer openings are surmounted by segmental pediments supported by brackets. The attic storey demonstrates how Michelangelo delights in breaking the rules: above the pilasters he places a small square block carved in low relief and flanked by inverted balusters.

The effigy of Giuliano is dressed in a close-fitting military tunic based on ancient Roman models and he holds a general's baton across his knees. The pose is similar to that of the *Moses*, as is the form of the drapery over the knees, but the inclined angle of the head gives the figure an altogether gentler character.

The two figures below represent *Night* (left), with her various attributes, notably the owl, and *Day*, a powerful giant whose unfinished face is somehow all the more expressive.

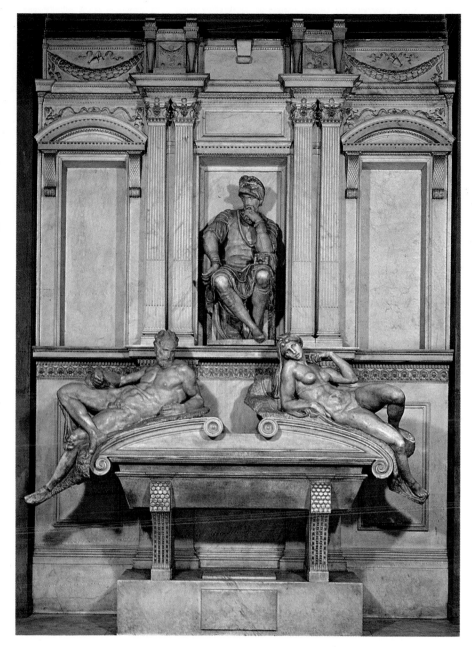

Above
The Tomb of Lorenzo de' Medici
1524–6
Florence: San Lorenzo

This commemorates Lorenzo, Duke of Urbino, who died in 1519, at the age of 28, and only a few weeks after his wife had died giving birth to a daughter Catherine, who was to become Queen of France and the mother of the last three Valois kings.

As Giuliano represents the active life supported by the positive times of night and day, so Lorenzo may be taken to represent the contemplative life, whose supporters are the indeterminate times of dawn and dusk. Lorenzo's face is shadowed by a huge helmet based on an Etruscan model and his mouth is hidden behind his hand as he gazes meditatively down into the space below. *Dawn*, like *Night*, is ostensibly female, although quite clearly both bodies are of young males with added breasts, pendulous and sagging in the former case, firm and high in the latter. *Dusk*, like *Day*, is a mature male, although his evident weariness contrasts with the latter's powerful alertness.

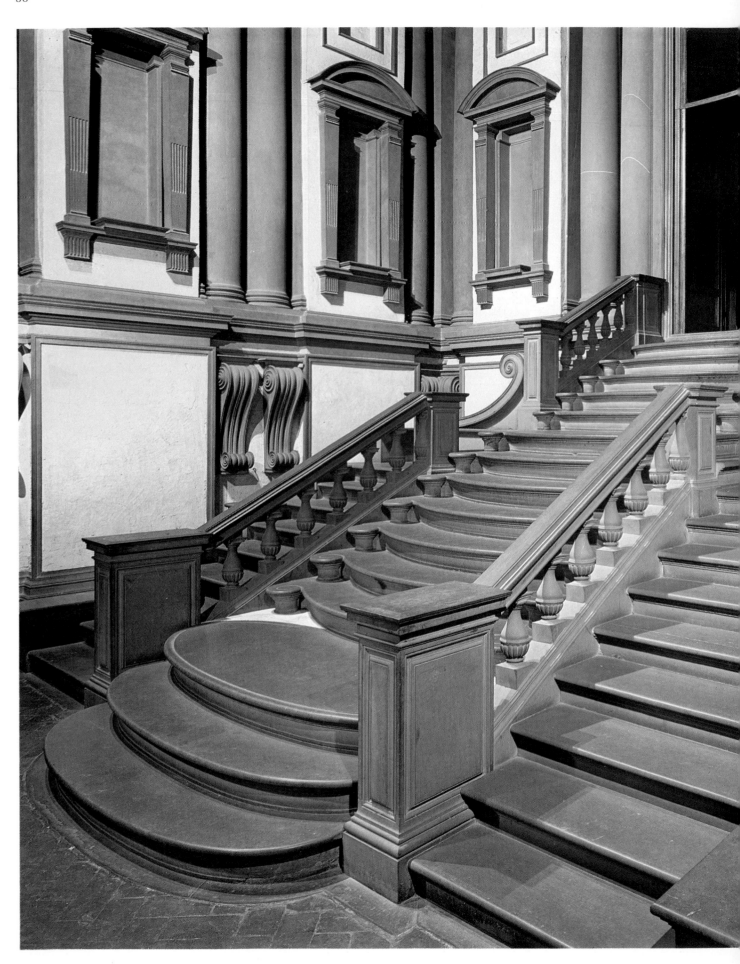

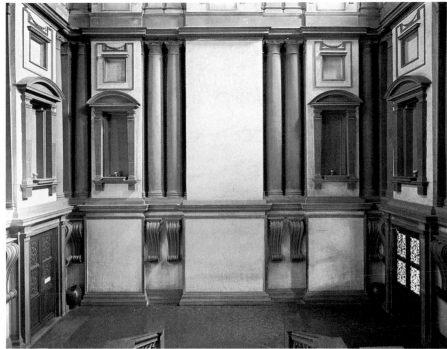

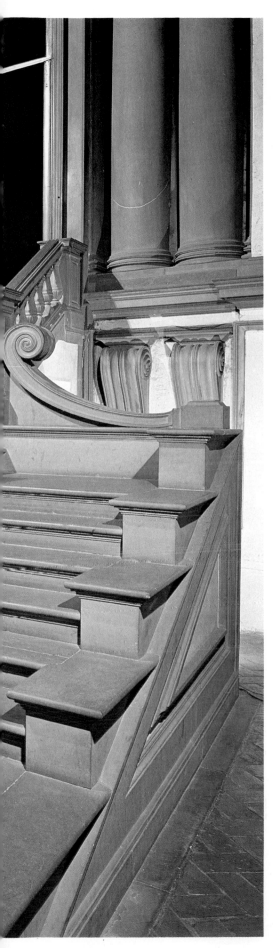

The Laurentian Library
Begun 1524
Florence: San Lorenzo

Even more than in the Medici Chapel, Michelangelo exploits the contrast between the dark stone (the famous *pietra serena*) and the whitened plaster of the walls, since the third element, marble, is no longer present.

The library, constructed above a range of existing monastic buildings, which had to be strengthened to bear the weight, consists of a long reading room, preceded by a vestibule. In the reading room the walls are split up by a giant order of stone pilasters. The space between these corresponds to that between the walnut reading desks (also designed by Michelangelo) whose height is that of the stone string course, which indicates the base from which the order rises. Thus architecture and furniture are perfectly integrated.

Much more controversial is the treatment of the vestibule (above), which is also dominated by an order, this time of columns which are set into recesses in the wall in pairs, flanked by wafer thin matching pilasters. Blank windows are framed by curious pilasters which are wider towards the top and support heavy pediments, either triangular or segmental. Below the coupled columns heavy brackets act as purely visual supports, since they serve no practical function whatsoever.

The most astonishing feature of the vestibule is, however, the staircase (left), completed in 1558–9 by Ammanati, apparently according to a design sent from Rome by Michelangelo, although the extent of his participation in its ultimate form has been questioned. It is undeniably eccentric, with its central flight based on a series of interlocking shallow ovals and the two outer flights not provided with any form of balustrade or handrail at the outer edge.

It is nevertheless brilliantly effective and in its theatricality it points the way towards those monumental stairways which are a prominent feature of the great baroque palaces of Germany.

Right
The Bearded Slave
Date unknown
Marble
255.5 cm (100½ in) high

Far right
The Awakening Slave
Date unknown
Marble
269.6 cm (106⅛ in) high
Florence: Accademia di Belle Arti

Alternatively called 'prisoners' or 'captives', these two are from a group of four which Michelangelo intended for the tomb of Julius II, as redefined in the 1516 contract. The blocks may well have been cut then, but there is no general agreement as to when the figures were brought to their present state, although some time during the 1520s seems probable.

After Michelangelo's death his nephew, Lionardo presented them to the Grand Duke Cosimo who later had them included in the famous Grotto by Buontalenti (1583) in the Boboli Gardens, where they have been replaced by casts.

Even in their unfinished state, it is clear that, unlike the two *Slaves* now in the Louvre, these were intended to support something, presumably a cornice, so that they are in fact atlantes, the male equivalent of caryatids. The *Bearded Slave* has been brought to a higher degree of finish, but probably only in part by Michelangelo, the legs especially suggesting the work of assistants. The *Awakening Slave*, intended as a corner figure, is still imprisoned in the marble, although enough of the figure has been released to justify the traditional title.

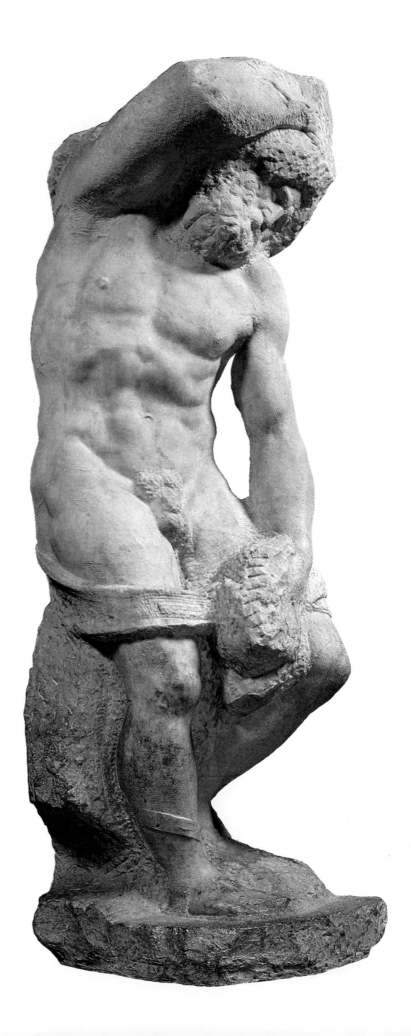

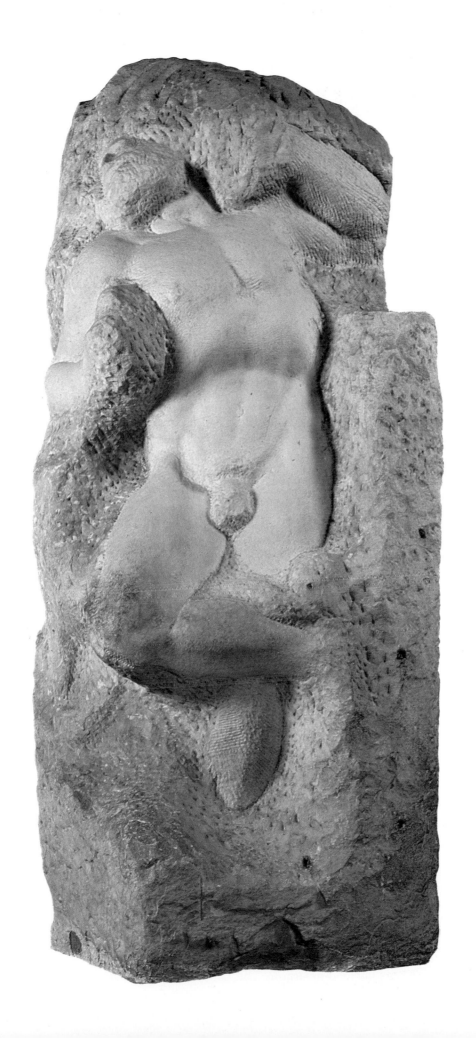

Friendship and Faith

The tangible result of Michelangelo's two intense personal relationships, with Cavalieri and Vittoria Colonna, was the group of highly finished drawings which have been called 'presentation drawings', since they were not intended as studies for other works but are complete in themselves. These demonstrate Michelangelo's phenomenal technique in any medium that he chose to employ – in this case chalk, either red or black. Having returned to Rome late in 1532, he wrote to Cavalieri in Rome on 1 January 1533, a day he describes as 'a happy day for me', since having written one letter he then received one from Cavalieri, to whom he immediately addressed another, dated the same day, in which he writes: 'if it is true that, as you write to me, you sincerely appreciate my works, if it so happens that I can make one as I wish, and you do like it, I will consider said work more fortunate than good'. With the two letters he enclosed a poem, in which, perhaps unconsciously recalling the imagery of the Sistine Chapel ceiling, he portrays Cavalieri as the sun, casting himself in the role of the moon:

'Your will includes and is the Lord of mine,
Life to my thoughts within your heart is given;
My works begin to breathe upon your breath;
Like to the moon am I, that cannot shine alone;
for lo! our eyes see nought in heaven save
what the living sun illuminate.'

The drawings that Michelangelo executed for Cavalieri are listed by Vasari, who describes them as 'many most superb drawings of divinely beautiful heads, designed in red and black chalk', adding that 'he drew for him a Ganymede rapt to Heaven by Jove's Eagle, a Tityus with the Vulture devouring his heart, the chariot of the sun falling with Phaethon into the Po, and a Bacchanal of children, which are all in themselves most rare things, and drawings the like of which had never been seen'. The *Rape of Ganymede* exists only in a copy in the royal collection in Great Britain, but the others have happily survived and are preserved at Windsor. Vasari also mentions a portrait of Cavalieri, which is now lost, but some idea of it may be derived from that of another young friend, Andrea Quaratesi, in the British Museum. The refinement of these drawings and their extraordinary degree of finish were immediately appreciated, as Vittoria Colonna recorded in her letter to Michelangelo on receipt of the superb *Christ on the Cross*.

When Michelangelo left Florence for good in September 1534, the statues for the Medici Chapel were still scattered about the floor and it was left to his assistants to supervise their installation: in Rome his childhood friend and patron, Pope Clement VII, lay on his deathbed, having commissioned from Michelangelo a *Resurrection* for the Sistine Chapel. His successor, Paul III Farnese, had other ideas, and it was for him that Michelangelo executed (1536–41) the tremendous *Last Judgement* that covers the altar wall of the Sistine Chapel whose ceiling he had painted nearly 30 years before. The sensation which it provoked at its unveiling was not wholly uncritical and, as time went on, the volume and intensity of opposition to Michelangelo's interpretation of his theme, almost exclusively by means of the nude, increased to such an extent that, barely a few months before he died, he was told that it was to be 'reformed' in accordance with the artistic policy set out at the Council of Trent. This led to the almost total banishment of the nude in religious art, unless it was absolutely necessary, as in a *Crucifixion*, although even here a little modest drapery was deemed desirable. The *Last Judgement*

An Ideal Head
Date unknown
Red chalk
20.5 × 16.5 cm (8 × 6½ in)
Oxford: Ashmolean Museum

Among the drawings made by Michelangelo for Cavalieri, Vasari mentions 'divinely beautiful heads', a description which may without hesitation be applied to this one. However, although Linda Murray accepts (with reservations) a dating of 1532–4, which would be appropriate chronologically, John Gere in his *Drawings by Michelangelo* catalogue (British Museum, 1975) states that the general view is that it is unlikely to be later than about 1525. This would rule out any link with Cavalieri.

In fact, it is very close in type to several of the *ignudi* on the Sistine Chapel ceiling, and so could date from as early as 1508–12, a possibility also accepted by Gere. The question of the sex of the sitter has been much discussed, but it seems safe with Michelangelo to assume that, without positive evidence to the contrary, it is male. The headdress, rightly described by Gere as 'a kind of fantastic helmet with cheek lappets', would tend to support this view, and the presence of the earring is inconclusive, since young men during the Renaissance were quite as likely to wear one, as they are today.

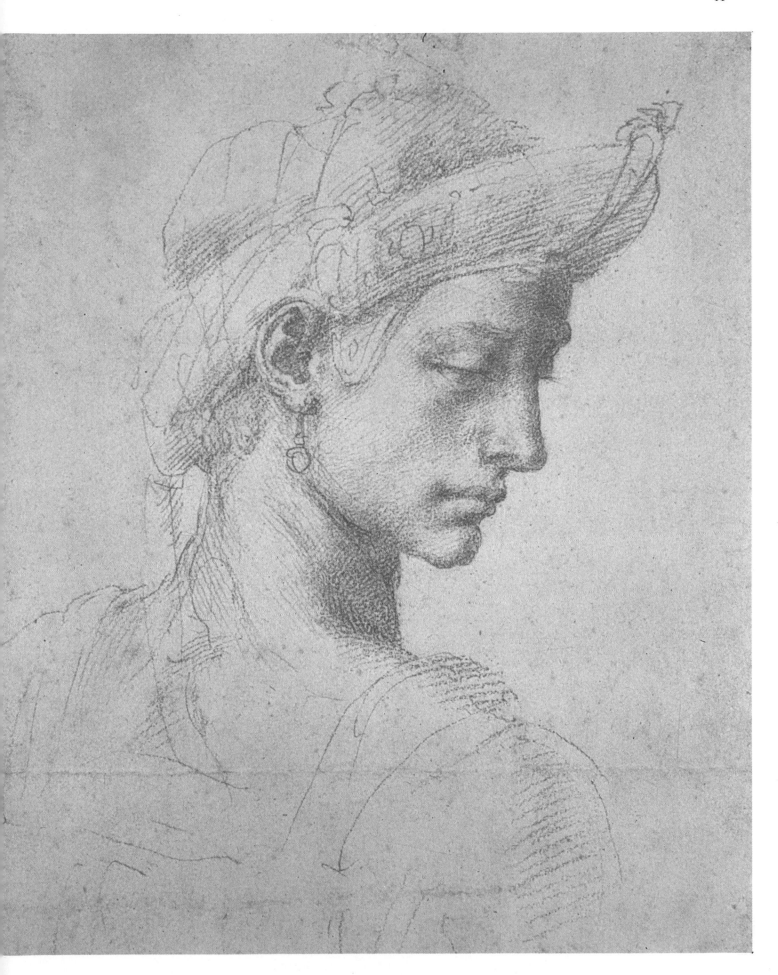

was accordingly made 'decent' by a team of painters, headed by Michelangelo's pupil, Daniele da Volterra, who was always known thereafter as 'the breeches maker'.

However, all this was to come, and in 1541 the Pope, Paul III, was so impressed with it that he immediately commissioned Michelangelo to paint two more frescoes, for his own private chapel, known as the Pauline Chapel: a *Conversion of St Paul* and a *Crucifixion of St Peter*. In the meantime the heirs of Julius II had seen the completion of the Tomb put off yet again, this time officially, by the Pope, who on 1 September 1535 had appointed Michelangelo 'supreme architect, sculptor and painter of the Apostolic Palace'. A year later the Pope absolved him from all obligations regarding the Tomb until he had finished the *Last Judgement*. In 1542 Michelangelo petitioned the Pope to release him from the 1532 Tomb contract, declaring that the two *Slaves* (now in the Louvre) were no longer appropriate to the modified design, for which a fifth (and final) contract was signed on 20 August 1542. Nevertheless it was to be another three years before the Tomb assumed its present unsatisfactory form in San Pietro in Vincoli.

Michelangelo never returned to Florence, but he was in regular touch with his family, principally his nephew Lionardo, whom he constantly berated for his incompetence and extravagance, even complaining in July 1540 that the shirts that the young man had sent him were 'so coarse that here you could not find a peasant who would not be ashamed to wear them'. He was also in contact with Florentine exiles in Rome, for the chief of whom, Donato Giannotti, he began work on a bust of Brutus to celebrate the assassination of the hated Duke Alessandro de' Medici in January 1536. He was succeeded by a member of a junior branch of the family, Cosimo, under whom the Duchy (later the Grand Duchy) prospered and for whom Michelangelo's biographer Vasari worked as artistic adviser and impresario.

Cosimo asked Michelangelo to make a bust of him but he declined on the grounds of old age (he was nearly 70) and failing eyesight. In any case he was deeply involved in Roman affairs, having undertaken in 1538 the remodelling of the *Campidoglio*, the motley collection of civic buildings on the Capitoline Hill, transforming it into an imposing, symmetrically disposed group of classical palaces centring on the ancient bronze statue of Marcus Aurelius. This figure had escaped the melting pot of the early Christian fanatics only because they had thought that it represented Constantine, the first Christian Emperor.

In 1546 the Pope appointed him architect of the family palace and of the most important building in Christendom, the new St Peter's. The original plan by Bramante had been considerably modified, notably by Antonio da Sangallo, but Michelangelo reverted to it, simplifying it somewhat, so that it acquired even greater monumentality. He worked on St Peter's without payment, 'for the love of God' and it is his deep religious faith that dominates all Michelangelo's late works, especially the two versions of the *Pietà*, in which he returned to the theme of his first great triumph at the very beginning of the century. This religious conviction is also reflected in his drawings of the Crucifixion, which, perhaps unconsciously, recall the monumentality of the frescoes by Masaccio that he had studied so avidly as a boy. In his last years he produced designs for the Laurentian Library staircase in Florence and for several buildings in Rome, including a remodelling of part of the Baths of Diocletian into a church, Santa Maria degli Angeli (altered out of all recognition in the 18th century), a chapel for Cardinal Sforza in Santa Maria Maggiore (built after Michelangelo's death by Giacomo della Porta) and the Porta Pia, begun for Pius IV in 1561.

Michelangelo died on 18 February 1564, in the presence of, among others, his beloved Cavalieri, and his body was taken, at the insistence of Duke Cosimo, to Florence, where it was buried in the church of Santa Croce. The memorial service in San Lorenzo was a state occasion attended by the leading citizens of the city and no fewer than 80 artists, including of course Vasari, who also designed the tomb in Santa Croce.

The Risen Christ
Date unknown
Black chalk
37.3 × 22.1 cm ($14\frac{11}{16} \times 8\frac{11}{16}$ in)
Windsor: Royal Library

Altogether 14 drawings in Michelangelo's own hand relating to the theme of the Resurrection survive.

They are usually dated to *c*.1532–3 and may have been produced to help Michelangelo's friend and pupil Sebastiano del Piombo (*c*.1485–1547), who in 1530 had been commissioned to paint an altarpiece of the *Resurrection* for the Chigi chapel in S. Maria della Pace, Rome. There he would have been in competition with Raphael's work, as he had been on an earlier occasion. This was in 1516, when his *Raising of Lazarus* (now in the National Gallery, London), for which Michelangelo had also supplied him with drawings, had had to compete with Raphael's *Transfiguration* (Vatican). Michelangelo's dislike of Raphael was basically what would today be called a clash of personalities and, although he seems to have avoided direct confrontation, he was quite prepared to challenge him through his own support for Sebastiano, even after his rival's early death (1520).

This drawing, one of the finest in the group, shows Christ rising dramatically from his tomb, at the same time casting off the shroud in which he was buried. The suggestion that it could be 20 years earlier than the others, connected with an unrealized project for an altarpiece on the theme of the *Resurrection*, which Pope Julius II was considering for the Sistine Chapel in 1516, is unacceptable in view of the close similarities between this and other drawings in the series.

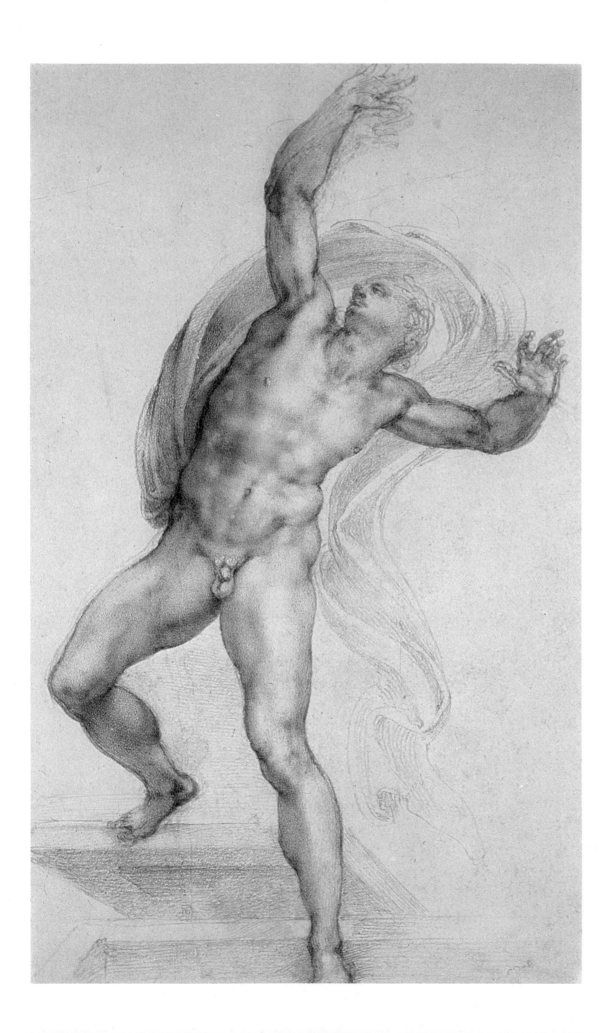

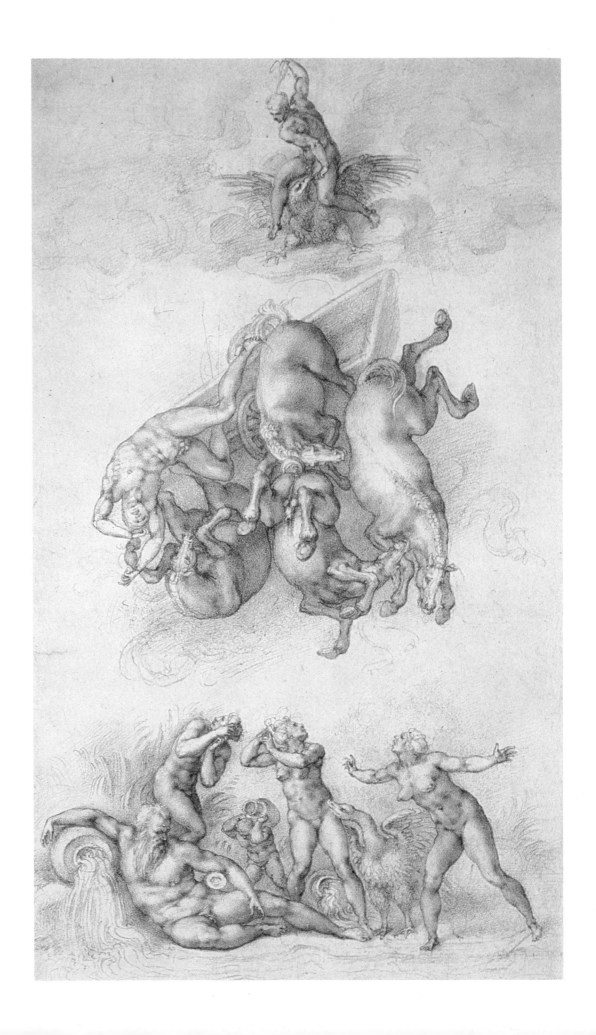

Left
The Fall of Phaethon
1533
Black chalk
41.3 × 23.4 cm (16¼ × 9⅜ in)
Windsor: Royal Library

This is one of the highly finished drawings that Vasari lists as having been produced for Tommaso de' Cavalieri. The enormous care that Michelangelo took over it is demonstrated by the existence of two preparatory studies, on one of which (now in the British Museum) he wrote a message to Cavalieri asking him whether he wished him to finish the drawing.

Phaethon, the son of Apollo, god of the sun, and a nymph, begged his father to allow him to drive the chariot of the sun across the skies. After much persuasion Apollo reluctantly agreed but Phaethon was unable to control the horses, which bolted, threatening to consume the earth with fire. A catastrophe was averted by Jupiter, who hurled a thunderbolt at the presumptuous young man, who fell from the heavens into the River Po.

In the drawing Jupiter on his eagle has just hurled the thunderbolt at Phaethon, who is thrown from the chariot, while below the Po is represented by a river god.

The three females are Phaethon's sisters who were punished for mourning their brother by being turned into poplar trees, and the swan their brother Cygnus, thus transformed.

The story is presumably an analogy of Michelangelo's own presumption in daring to love Cavalieri, whom he calls his 'sun' in one of his sonnets.

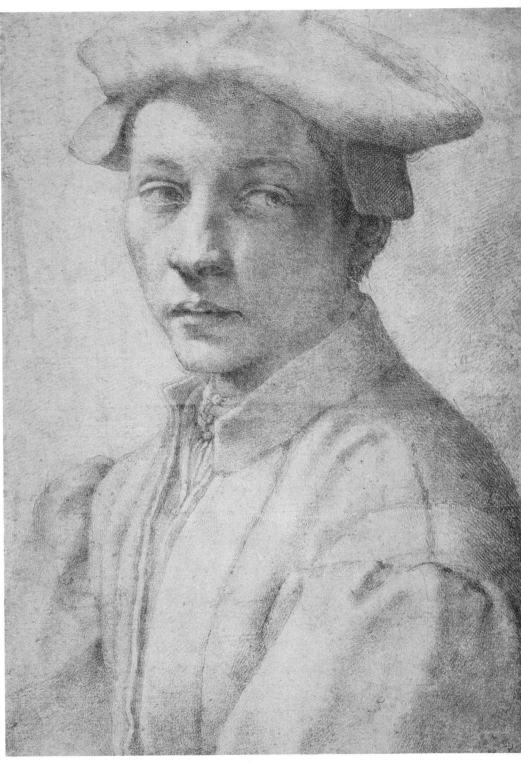

Andrea Quaratesi
1532
Black chalk
41.1 × 29.2 cm (16³⁄₁₆ × 11½ in)
London: British Museum

Of the four recorded versions, this is accepted as the original, executed in Florence in 1532.

The sitter is Andrea di Rinieri Quaratesi, a member of a noble Florentine family, with whom Michelangelo was on friendly terms. He is shown at the age of about 20.

This is the only portrait drawing by Michelangelo to survive, as one of Cavalieri, described by Vasari as 'a life-size portrait . . . in a cartoon' (black chalk) has disappeared. As Vasari also pointed out, Michelangelo rarely made portraits, 'because he abhorred executing a resemblance to the living subject unless it were of extraordinary beauty'.

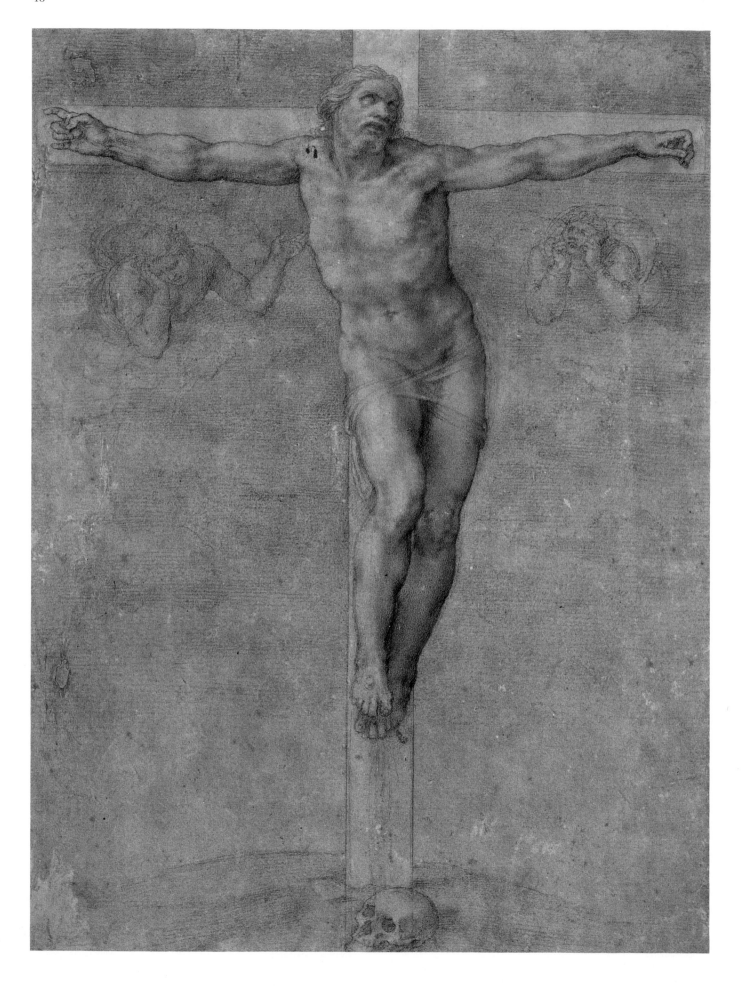

Left
Christ on the Cross
*c.*1540
Black chalk
37 × 27 cm (14⅝ × 10⅝ in)
London: British Museum

This superb drawing is usually identified as one of three that Michelangelo executed for his only close female friend, Vittoria Colonna, Marchesa di Pescara (1492–1547). After the death of her husband at the Battle of Pavia (1525), she devoted herself to religion.

Christ's upturned eyes and parted lips would suggest that Michelangelo has chosen to depict the most poignant moment of the crucifixion, when Christ momentarily doubts, calling upon his Father: 'My God, my God, why hast thou foresaken me.'

Writing to thank him for this drawing, Vittoria Colonna enthuses: 'It is not possible to see an image better made, more alive and more finished and certainly I could not explain how subtly and marvellously wrought it is . . . I have looked at it carefully in the light, with the glass, and with the mirror and I have never seen a more finished thing.'

Below
Brutus
*c.*1540
Marble
74 cm (29⅛ in) high (without base)
Florence: Museo Nazionale (Bargello)

Michelangelo's youthful gratitude to the Medici had gradually over the years turned into an obsessive hatred of the family as the destroyers of Florence's republican liberty. The first Duke, Alessandro, who was probably an illigitimate son of Pope Clement VII although he claimed Lorenzo, Duke of Urbino as his father, was murdered in 1537 by his cousin Lorenzaccio.

Ironically, the bust was acquired after Michelangelo's death by the Grand Duke Francesco de' Medici who had an inscription carved on it claiming that the artist had left the work unfinished, because he realized that he was commemorating a murder. This sounds more like an official gloss than the truth.

Nevertheless, the bust is unfinished and, although the face has been brought virtually to completion, the hair has merely been roughed out. The draperies were largely re-worked by Michelangelo's pupil, Tiberio Calcagni, to whom he gave it.

In its uncompromising severity, the *Brutus* is a telling embodiment of patriotic heroism.

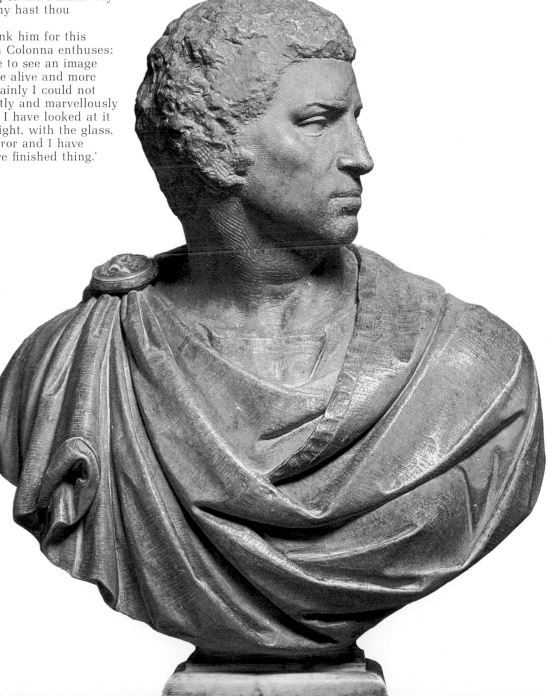

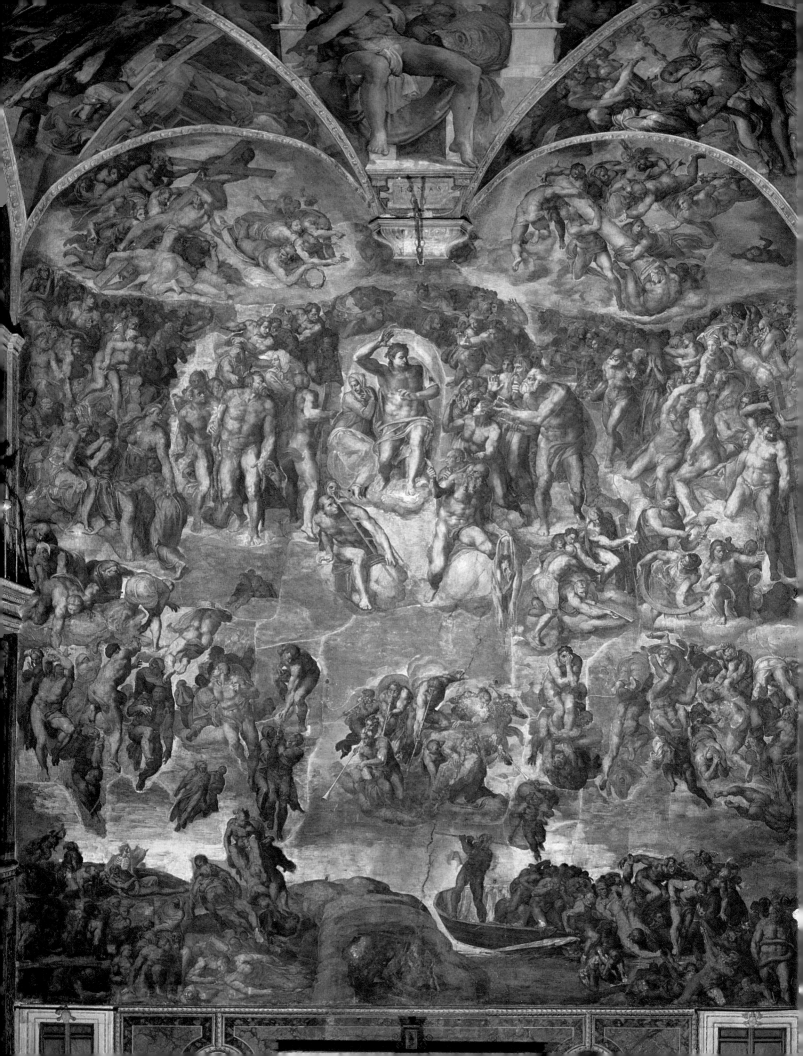

Left
The Last Judgement
1536–41
Fresco
13.7 × 12.2 metres (45 × 40 ft)
Rome: Vatican, Sistine Chapel, wall
above the altar

Depictions of the Last Judgement are
relatively rare, perhaps because of
the demands inherent in the subject,
which by definition must be on the
grandest scale. The end of the world
has to be convincingly depicted
with, as its focus, Christ himself
portrayed rewarding the saved and
punishing the damned. Earlier
attempts which Michelangelo might
have studied are those by Giotto in
the Scrovegni Chapel, Padua, and by
Luca Signorelli in the Cathedral at
Orvieto, the latter of which provides
the closest parallels with the Sistine
Chapel, especially in its exploitation
of the nude.

Christ, a huge figure more like
Hercules than 'gentle Jesus, meek
and mild', towers over the whole
composition, which is based on a
circular movement, beginning at the
lower left. There, summoned by
seven angelic trumpeters, the dead
rise from their graves and are
brought to the seat of judgement. A
swirling mass of souls rises up and
moves behind the central group of
Christ, the Virgin and the Saints, the
saved joining the ranks of the
blessed while the damned are hurled
down on the right towards Charon,
the boatman of Hell, who is waiting
to ferry them to eternal torment.

Michelangelo's nudes here become
heavier, and more powerful and his
colours more sombre in accordance
not only with his apocalyptic theme,
but also with his own changed
personality. At over 60 years old, his
intense sensuality has become an
equally intense obsession with death.

Details from The Last Judgement
Right
St Bartholomew

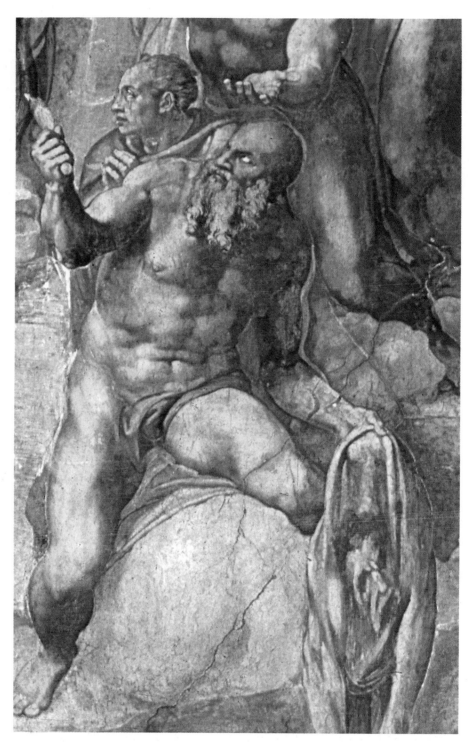

On either side of Christ and the
Virgin are grouped saints who have
been martyred for their faith. They
press forward, holding out the
instruments of their suffering and
death. Prominent among them,
seated on a cloud just below Christ's
feet, is the figure of St Bartholomew,
clutching in his right hand the knife
with which he was flayed alive. In
his left he holds his own skin,
which on closer examination
assumes the features of
Michelangelo himself.

Overleaf
Charon and the damned

The scene at the bottom right-hand
corner shows Charon, the boatman
of Hell, ferrying the souls of the
damned across the River Styx.

He raises his oar in a threatening
gesture, driving his passengers into
the arms of demons who are waiting
to drag them down to the bottomless
pit. The composition of this closely
packed group of originally totally
nude figures is developed from the

Deluge on the ceiling and ultimately
the *Cartoon of Pisa*.

The figure on the extreme right,
with the ass's ears and a serpent
entwined around his body, is Minos,
Prince of Hell. Michelangelo gave
him the features of the Pope's
interfering Chamberlain Biagio da
Cesena.

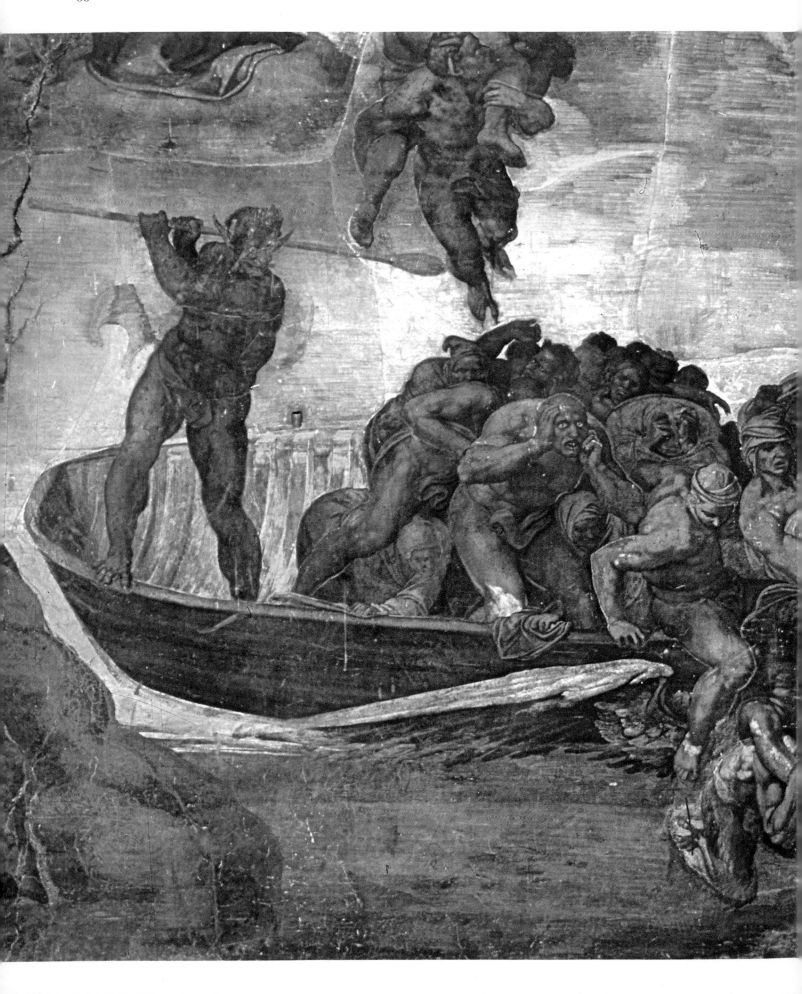

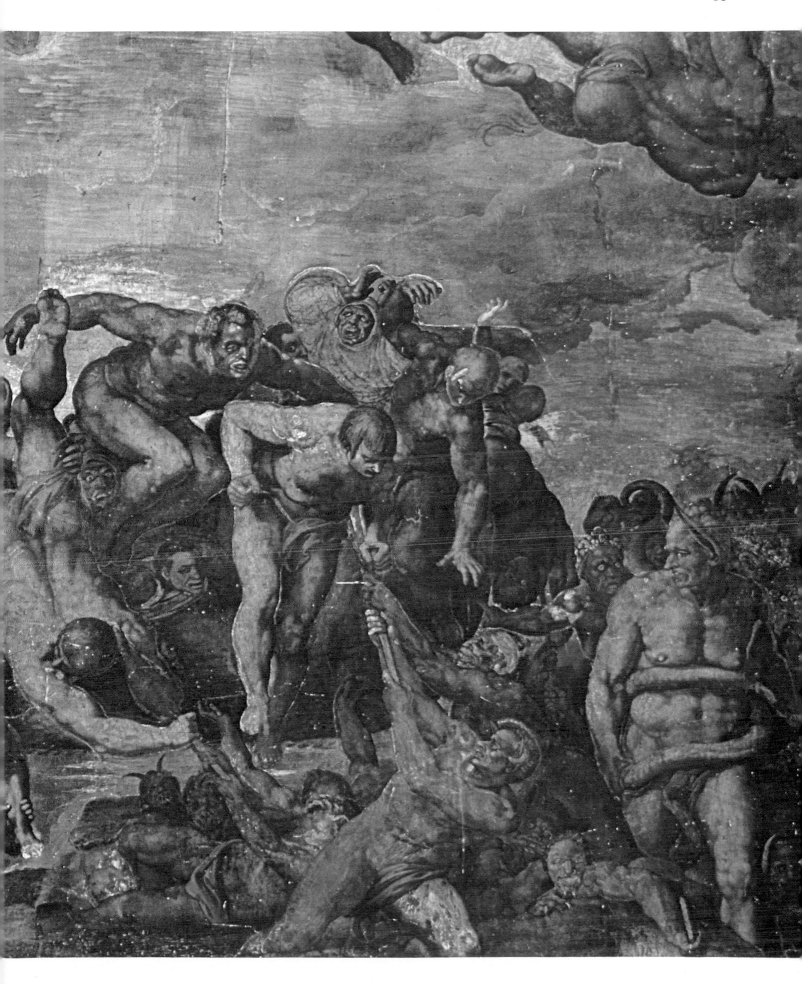

Below
The Conversion of St Paul
1542–5

Below right
The Crucifixion of St Peter
1546–50
Fresco
Both 6.25 × 6.61 metres
(20 ft 6 in × 21 ft 9 in)
Rome: Vatican, Pauline Chapel

Pope Paul III commissioned Antonio da Sangallo to build him, not far from the Sistine Chapel, a private chapel which was under construction from about 1537. As soon as the *Last Judgement* was completed, the Pope set Michelangelo to work painting the side walls of this chapel in fresco.

On the left-hand side facing the altar is depicted the *Conversion of St Paul*. Saul of Tarsus, an enthusiastic persecutor of Christians, was travelling to Damascus in search of further victims when he was struck down by a flash of divine lightning. This made him blind for three days as well as converting him instantly to the faith that he had sought to root out. He became one of the most important missionaries of the early Church, being considered, with St Peter, as one of its real founders.

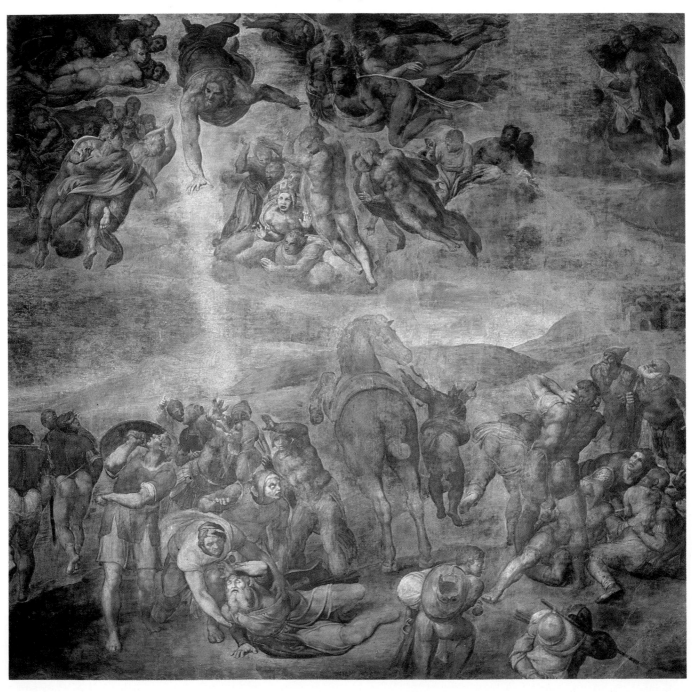

Paul (as he became) is made the central figure in the foreground, where, blind and having fallen from his horse, he is helped up by a servant. Although he was still a man in his prime, he has been given by Michelangelo the features of the aged Pope, who was to die before the completion of the programme of decoration. Christ appears above, in steep foreshortening, surrounded by angels, while below Paul's attendants react variously and one leads away his frightened horse.

For the opposite wall, the Pope had originally chosen as the subject *Christ giving the keys to St Peter*, but instead he decided on the *Crucifixion of St Peter*. The saint was crucified upside down, at his own request, out of respect for Christ, and he is shown already nailed to his cross, which the executioners are raising into position supervised by a group of Roman soldiers. The huge figure in yellow on the extreme right is usually thought to be a self-portrait.

In both frescoes, as in the *Last Judgement*, the composition is based on a circular motion, although there are otherwise marked differences. The colours are much less harsh, recalling the warmer tones of the Sistine Chapel ceiling and there is a marked absence of nude figures.

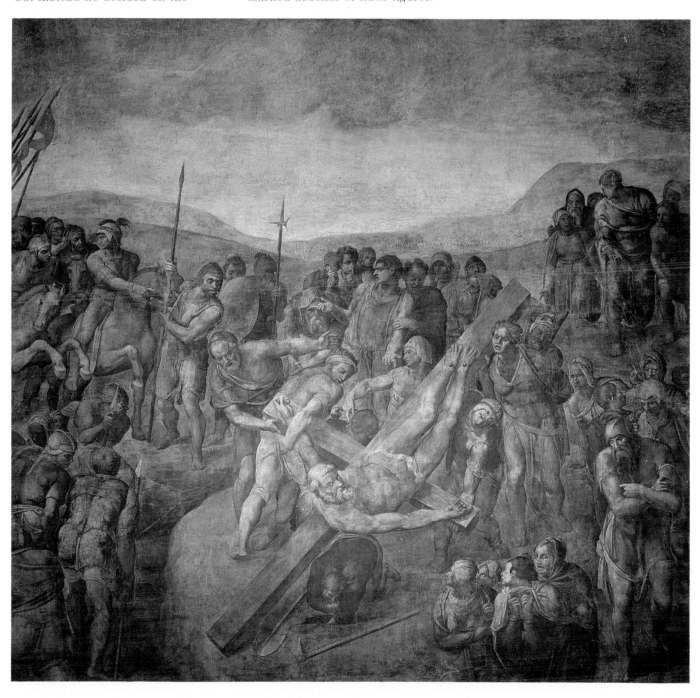

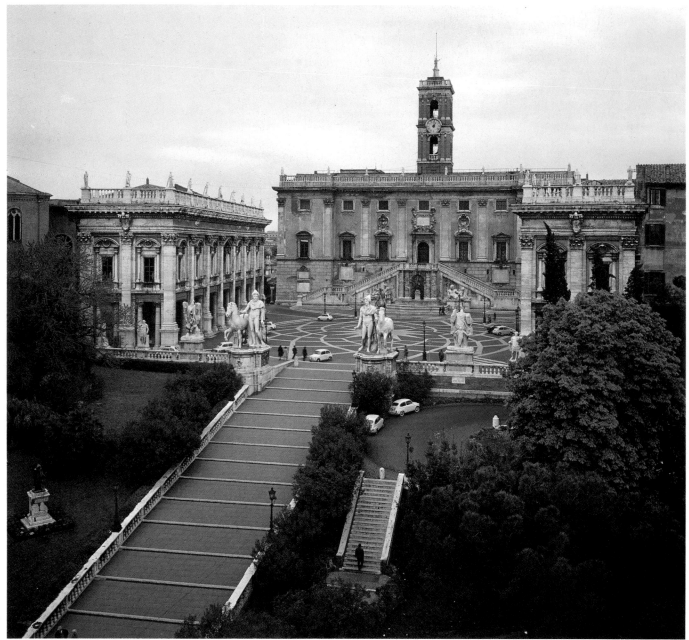

Piazza del Campidoglio
Designed 1538
Rome: Capitoline Hill

Michelangelo's earlier architectural achievements, notably the Medici Chapel and the Laurentian Library, were basically additions to the existing structures which from the outside are either inconspicuous or even invisible.

The buildings on the Capitoline Hill symbolized what remained of Roman municipal authority: in the centre was the palace of the one surviving senator, the Palazzo del Senatore, and to the right (when facing it) the palace of the councillors, the Palazzo dei Conservatori. On the Pope's instructions, Michelangelo placed the ancient bronze equestrian statue of Marcus Aurelius in the centre of the open space, on a new pedestal which he designed for it. A little later he produced a scheme for the piazza which is preserved in an engraving by Étienne Dupérac (1568): the Palazzo dei Conservatori is shown refronted in classical style, with an identical building constructed at the opposite side, even though there was no practical need for it. At the same time the Palazzo del Senatore was to be tidied up by the rebuilding in the centre of its tower, formerly slightly to one side.

All this proceeded slowly, mostly after Michelangelo's death, and his design for the pavement was not in fact carried out until 1940.

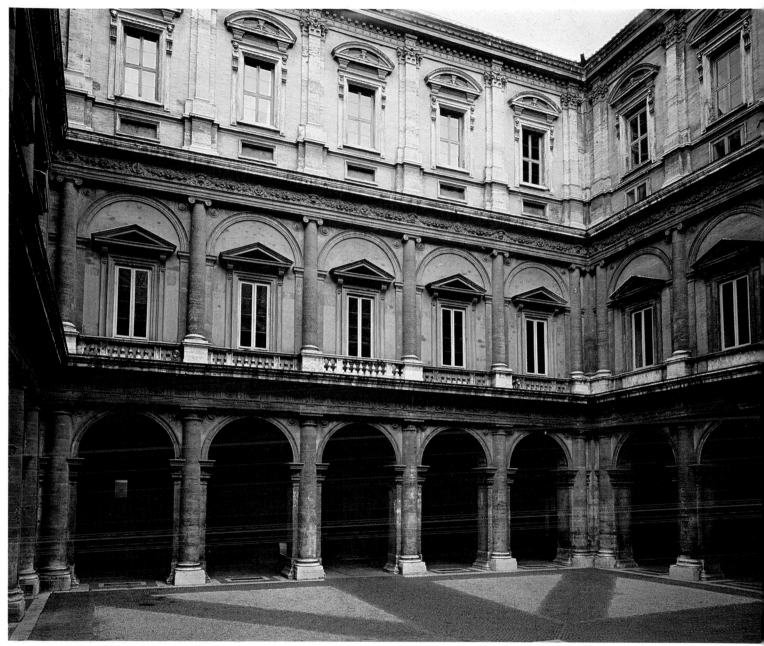

Palazzo Farnese, courtyard
Rome: Piazza Farnese

The Roman Palace of the Farnese family was begun by Antonio da Sangallo for Cardinal Alessandro Farnese in 1517, who became Pope Paul III in 1534. The main façade had reached the second (top) floor by the time Sangallo died in 1546, and Michelangelo was mainly responsible for the imposing cornice that crowns the building.

The interior courtyard had not proceeded so far and he was able to design the second floor himself. While observing the use of the orders as demonstrated by the Colosseum (Doric on the ground floor, Ionic on the first, Corinthian on the second) he abandoned the scheme of arcades and used pilasters instead of columns. He also managed to insert a mezzanine floor, giving his order a high base in order to accommodate it. The heavy segmental pediments over the windows are a visual reminder of the arcading below as well as acting as a counter-balance to the strong lines of the powerful cornice above.

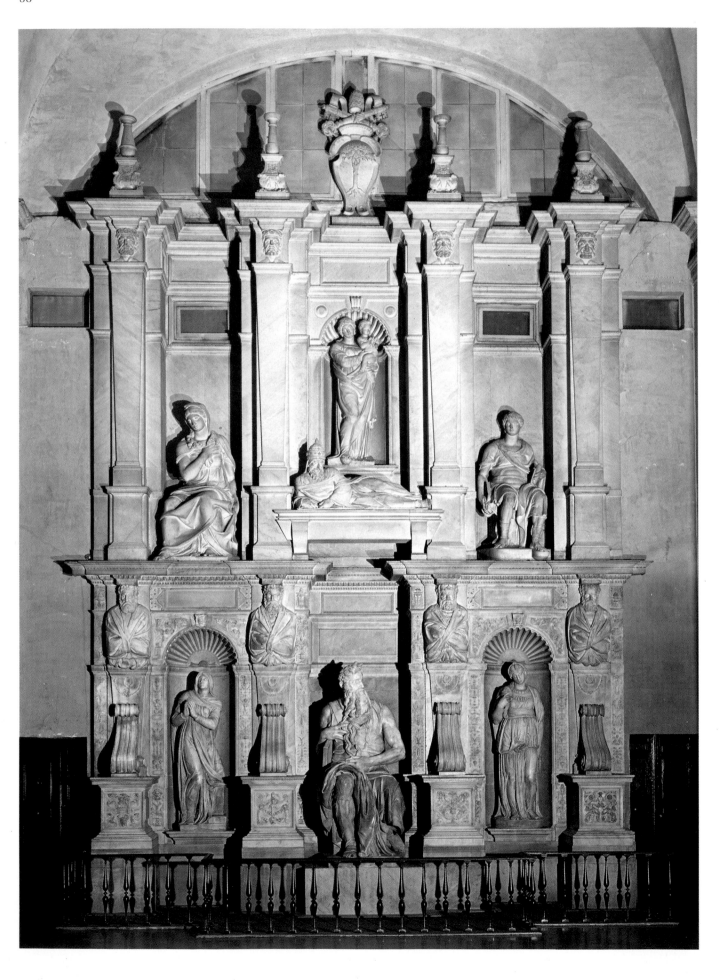

Left
The Tomb of Pope Julius II
Completed 1547
Marble
Rome: San Pietro in Vincoli

What Condivi called the 'tragedy of
the tomb' ended in this anticlimax,
which a recent writer goes so far as
to call a 'miserable object'.

Apart from the *Moses*, it is
certainly thoroughly unsatisfactory,
both in composition which is virtually
a parody of the Medici tombs in San
Lorenzo, and as regards the
statuary. Although the figures of
Rachel and *Leah* which flank the
Moses are largely by Michelangelo,
they are, for him, relatively
undistinguished, perhaps, as has
been somewhat cynically suggested,
because they are clothed and female.
The other figures are little short of
disastrous and Michelangelo had
little to do with them apart from
indicating their subject and general
form, including the curious reclining
effigy of the Pope which is based on
ancient Etruscan funeral
monuments.

It is not surprising that the Della
Rovere family were extremely
unhappy with the result and felt
that they had been cheated.

Right and overleaf
St Peter's, Rome
Vatican

Pope Julius II's determination to
leave a lasting memorial to himself
led not only to the commission to
Michelangelo for the grandiose tomb
that was to plague the artist for 40
years, but also to the construction of
the building originally intended to
house it. In 1506 the Basilica of St
Peter, built by the Emperor
Constantine in the fourth century,
was demolished and a new building
begun to the designs of Donato
Bramante (1444–1514), a man whom
Michelangelo disliked intensely,
although when he reluctantly agreed
to accept responsibility for St Peter's
he scrupulously respected his plans.

This had not been the case with
the other architects who at various
times had been called in,
particularly Antonio da Sangallo,
who spent seven years and a small
fortune producing an enormous
model of his own design, which
Michelangelo denounced as totally
inappropriate.

He therefore demolished those
parts that Sangallo had begun
which did not accord with

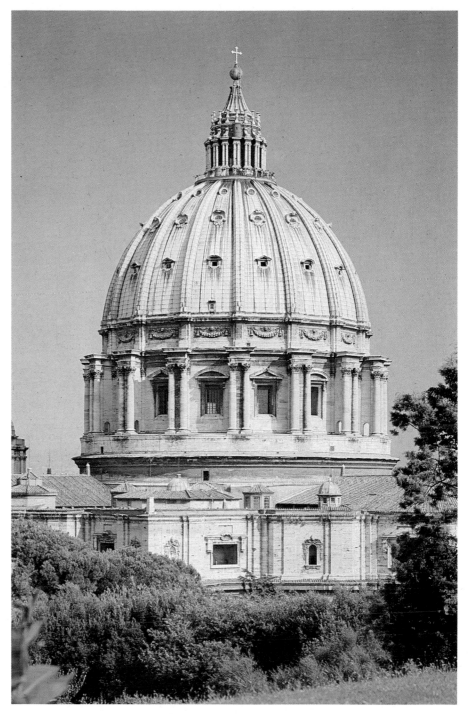

Bramante's plan. He did however
simplify the design, as well as
accepting the increased dimensions
of the four central piers proposed by
Sangallo.

By the time of Michelangelo's
death the construction of the great
building had reached the top of the
drum of the dome, whose
construction was undertaken by
Giacomo della Porta. He modified the
hemispherical outline intended by
Michelangelo, mainly for structural
reasons. It is on the 'hidden' side of
the building that Michelangelo's
work can best be appreciated: his

giant order of pilasters, reminiscent
of the Palazzo dei Conservatori,
creates a powerful vertical
movement which transcends the
huge mass of the structure to
culminate in the dome above.

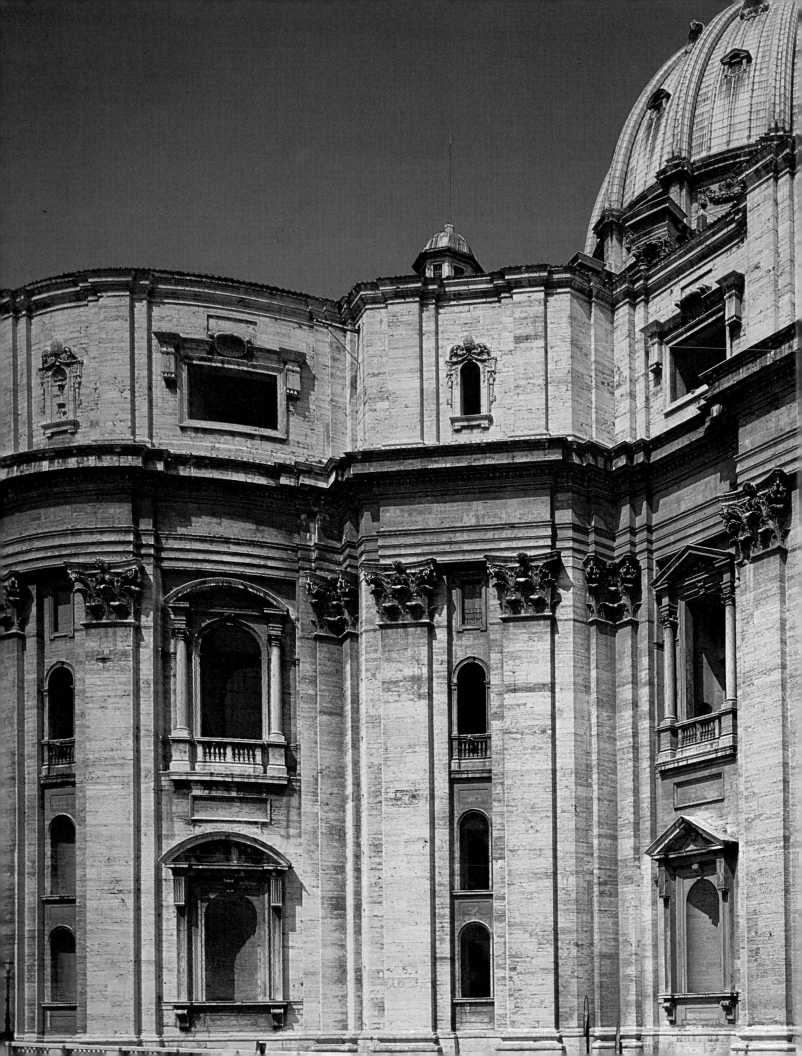

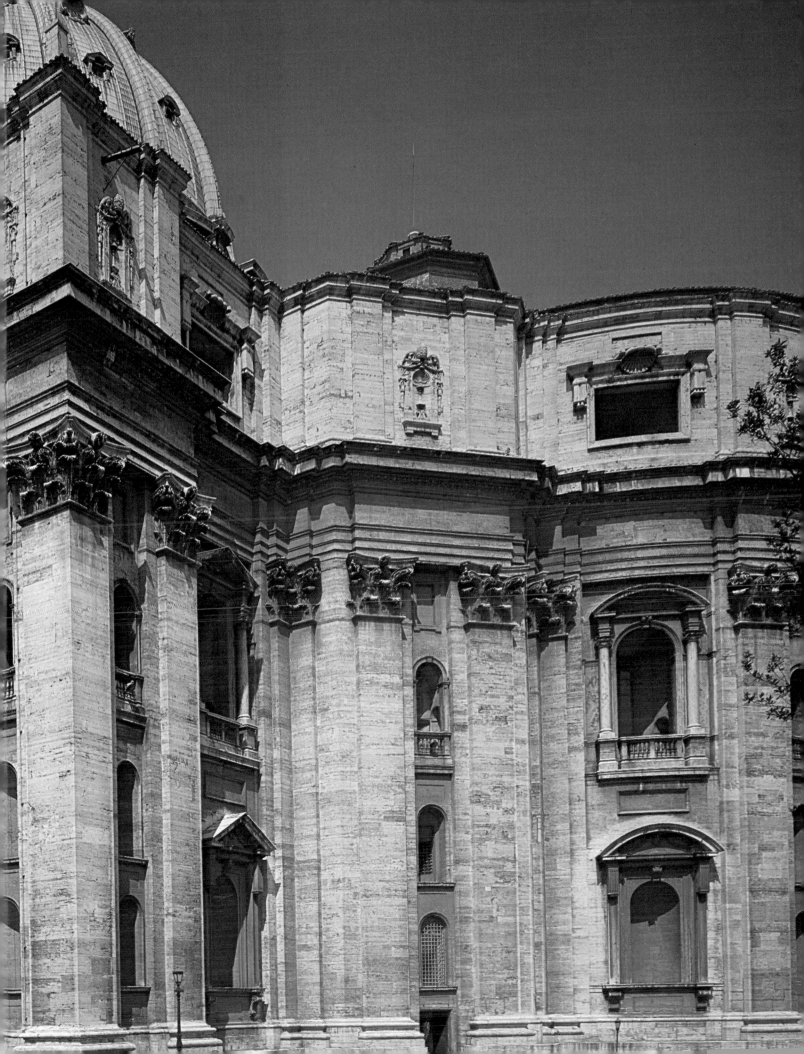

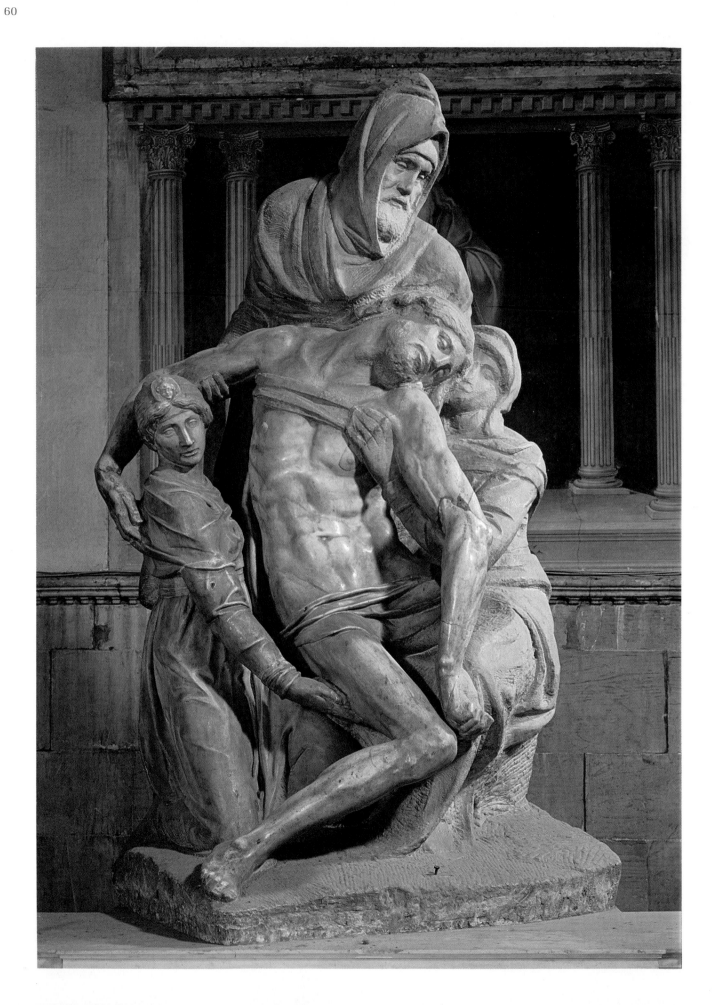

Left
The Florence Pietà
c.1547–55
Marble
226 cm (89 in) high
Florence: Cathedral (Santa Maria del
Fiore)

This group, unfinished and
mutilated as it is, is one of
Michelangelo's most moving
achievements, and was almost
certainly intended for his own tomb.
It has been in Florence since the
17th century, and in the cathedral
from 1721.

It may have been begun after the
death of Vittoria Colonna (1547),
which grieved Michelangelo deeply,
or, as Alessandro Parronchi (1969)
suggests, it could even have been
begun as early as 1534–5 for a papal
tomb. It remained unfinished in the
artist's studio and was damaged by
him in a moment of dissatisfaction.
He was prevented from destroying it
however, and his pupil Tibero
Calcagni managed to repair it. He
also completed the figure of the
Magdalen on the left and intended
to replace the missing left leg of
Christ, which at one time belonged
to Daniele da Volterra but is now
lost.

The contrast with the Rome Pietà,
completed half a century before,
could hardly be greater. The
deliberate awkwardness of Christ's
pose and the avoidance of obvious
physical beauty go back beyond the
Renaissance to the intense,
tormented spirituality of the Middle
Ages.

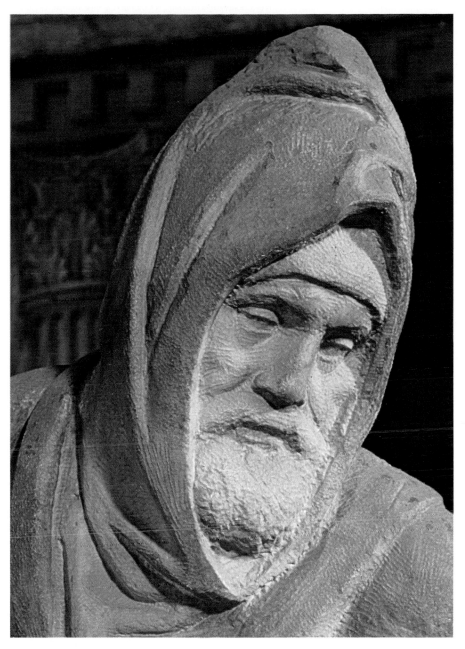

Detail from The Florence Pietà

Above
The head of Nicodemus (or Joseph of
Arimathea)

The hooded figure standing at the
rear of the Pietà has the
unmistakable features of the aged
Michelangelo, but there is some
doubt as to whether it is meant to
be Nicodemus or Joseph of
Arimathea.

Frederick Hartt (1969), who gives
the matter careful consideration,
comes to the conclusion that it is
more likely to be Joseph of
Arimathea, who gave his own tomb
to the dead Christ. Nicodemus,
however, helped to carry the body to
the tomb and was traditionally

believed to be a sculptor, so that
there is a case to be made for both
identifications.

In fact, such a consideration is of
minor importance. What matters is
the poignancy and beauty of the
artist's last portrait of himself, tired,
infinitely sad and utterly
disillusioned with a world that he
seems only too ready to leave. There
is even a hint of bitterness in the
downward twist of the tightly
compressed lips.

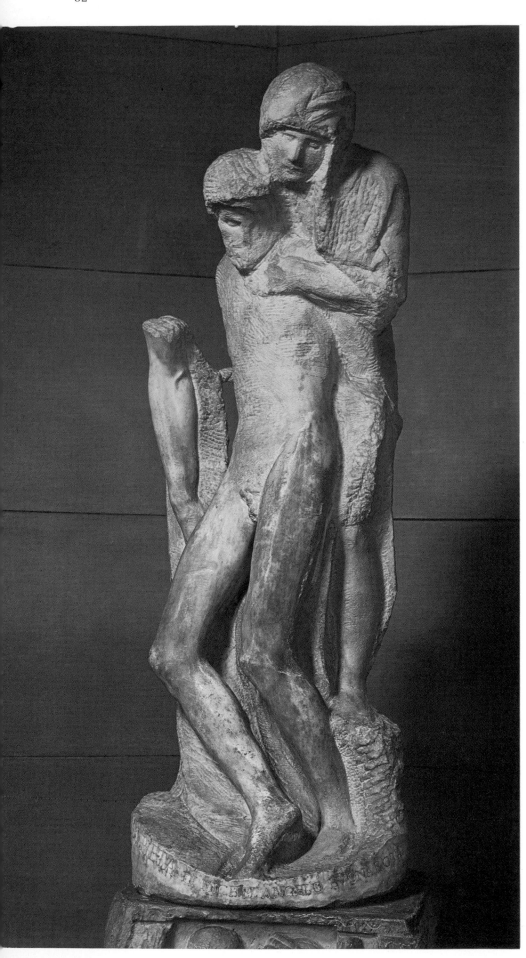

The Rondanini Pietà
1555–64
Marble
195 cm (76¾ in) high
Milan: Castello Sforzesco

So called because it was for many years in the Rondanini Palace in Rome, this shattered group (damaged like the *Florence Pietà* by Michelangelo himself) was in the artist's studio at his death.

The idea of a *Deposition*, with the dead Christ supported by either one or two figures, is recorded in a drawing (Oxford, Ashmolean Museum) of about 1555, that Linda Murray relates to this Pietà, although she admits, the inherent improbability of the Virgin, who is supporting the dead Christ, being represented 'with one stalwart leg bare to the knee'.

An ingenious, if not entirely convincing explanation is put forward by Alessandro Parronchi in the catalogue of the exhibition of religious art held at the church of Santo Stefano al Ponte, Florence, in the context of the Council of Europe *Medici* exhibition (1980). There a fragment of a head and shoulder of Christ (59 cm/23¼ in high) was displayed, in conjunction with casts of the *Pietà*, to which it certainly seems to relate. Parronchi's theory is that the original design was for a dead Christ supported by angels with the Virgin standing behind, her arms outstretched, and that it was begun for Vittoria Colonna. It would then pre-date the *Florence Pietà*. Such a conjecture, while stimulating, does not impinge upon the work itself, in which calm and resignation seem to have taken possession of the artist's soul, as if to compensate for the enfeebled state of his body.

Right
**Christ on the Cross between the
Virgin and St John**
c.1560
Black chalk (with white paint used
for corrections)
41.2 × 27.9 cm (16¼ × 11 in)
London: British Museum

Such later drawings testify to
Michelangelo's increasing obsession
with death and his hope of
salvation. They are also, like the
Rondanini Pietà, a pathetic
testimony to his physical
deterioration.

The outlines of the massive figure
are blurred and made up of several
marks on the paper and he has used
white paint to make corrections. The
figures themselves derive from those
in the *Last Judgement* and the
frescoes in the Pauline Chapel but,
interestingly, he has returned to his
abiding passion, the male nude. This
would seem an argument against the
idea that they are in any sense
'presentation drawings'. They are
surely intensely private, personal
statements by an old man still
seeking to reconcile the
contradictions in his art and his
own nature.

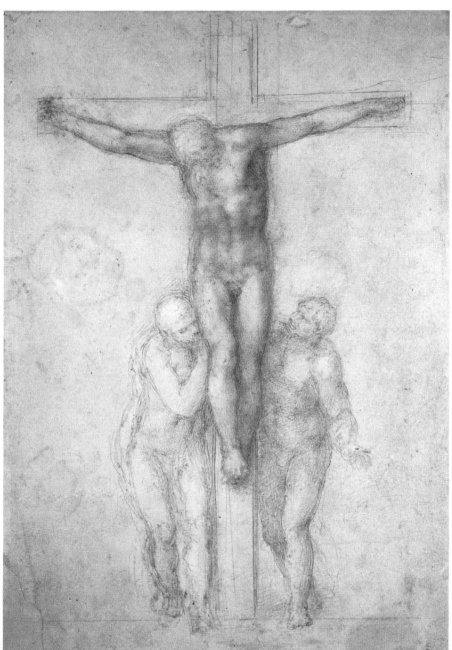

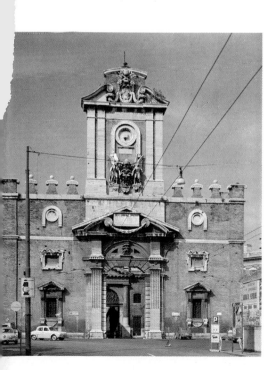

Left
Porta Pia, Rome
1561–5

Michelangelo designed this gate for
Pope Pius IV, at the point where his
new road, the via Pia, breached the
walls of Rome.

The construction does not follow
the design in every detail and the
upper stage, which was rebuilt in
1853, replaces Michelangelo's simple
triangular pediment by a much more
elaborate 'broken' type which
anticipates the Baroque style.

Nevertheless, the essentials are
his, as an engraving by Faleti (1568)
proves. The ground floor windows
are of the 'kneeling' type, supported
on brackets, that he had devised for
the Medici palace (c.1517), while the
blank windows above recall the
openings at the attic level, above the
cornice, of St Peter's. The doorway is
extraordinary, consisting of a
canted, flattened opening, like the
plan of a bay window, surmounted
by a segmental arch and then
topped by two pediments, a curved,
broken one fitted inside a triangular
one. In addition, the ornamentation
is treated as three different levels or
layers. The absence of the obelisks
planned by Michelangelo to
surmount the pilaster strips at the
outer edges is particularly
unfortunate, as they would have
helped to balance the
disproportionately tall and narrow
upper storey.

Index

Numbers in *italics* refer to captions

Acknowledgements

The publishers wish to thank the following organizations and individuals for their kind permission to reproduce the photographs in this book:
Reproduced by gracious permission of Her Majesty the Queen (Royal Library, Windsor) 43, 44; Accademia, Florence (Scala) front cover, 12, 13, 16 left, 38, 39; Ashmolean Museum 41; Bargello, Florence (Scala) 1, 10, 16 right, 47; British Museum 26 below, 45, 46, 63 right; Bruges Cathedral (Scala) 15; Casa Buonarroti, Florence (Scala) 7, 8, 9 above; Castello Sforzesco (Scala) 62; Duomo, Florence (Scala) 60, 61; Holkham Hall (Angelo Hornak) 18; Laurentian Library, Florence (Scala) 36–37; Musée du Louvre, Paris (Scala) 31; Medici Chapel, Florence (Scala) 33, 34, 35; Metropolitan Museum of Art, New York (Joseph Pulitzer Bequest, Purchase 1924) 24; The National Gallery, London 19; Pauline Chapel, Vatican (Scala) 52, 53; The Royal Academy 17; S. Maria sopra Minerva, Rome (Scala) 32 left; S. Pietro in Vincoli, Rome (Scala) 29, 56; San Procolo, Bologna (Scala) 9 below; St. Peter's Basilica, Rome (Scala) 11; Scala 54, 55, 57, 58–9; Scala/Hamlyn Picture Library 63 left; Sistine Chapel, Vatican (Scala) 2–3, 4–5, 20–1, 22–3, 25, 26–7, 48, 49, 50–1; Uffizi Gallery, Florence (Scala) 14, back cover; Vecchio Palace, Florence (Scala) 32 right.

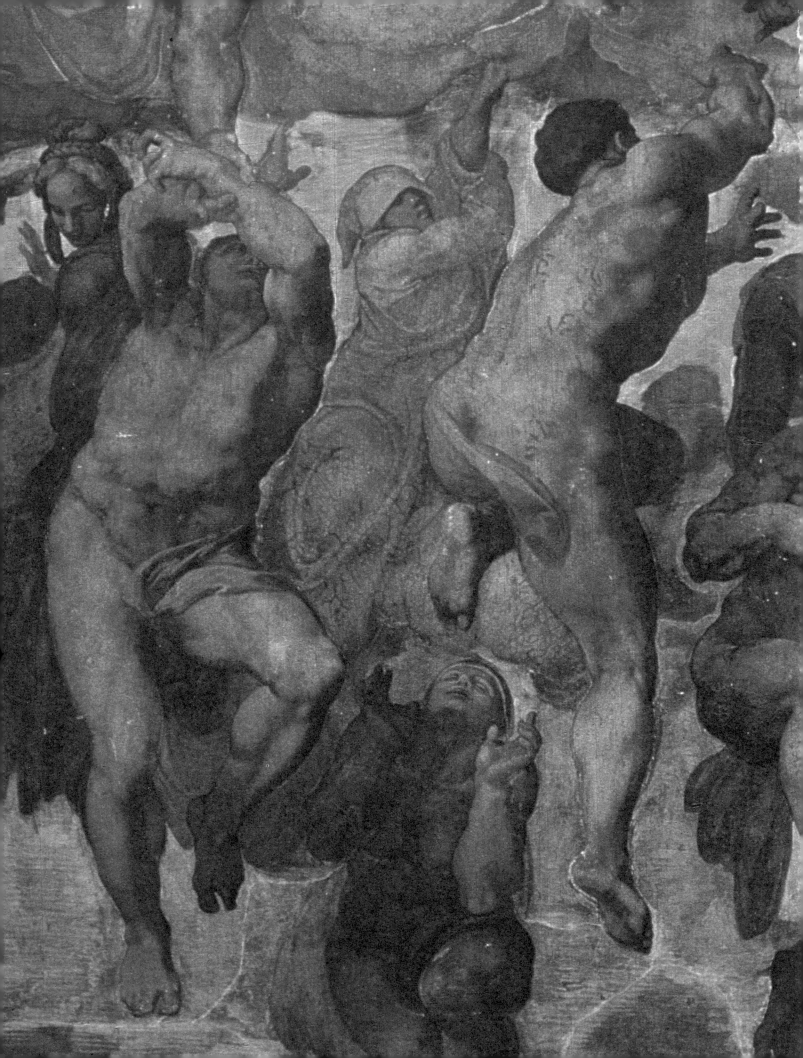